This book is for
Linbert, Matthew
and Daniel.

Acknowledgements

I would like to thank the teachers, carers, social workers and medical staff who have helped and supported us as a family over the years. Special thanks go to my parents, sister and her family who have given so generously of their time and love and so often gone the extra mile. To Matt, for not only surviving as a sibling to Daniel, but for thriving against all odds, for maintaining his sense of humour and becoming a gracious, caring person. Last, but never least, is Linbert who apart from bearing the burden of editing and fine tuning my inadequate computer skills has supported me through all our years with Daniel and without whom I could not have coped.

CONTENTS

Foreword

Dear Reader

Daniel is one of the most unique human beings I have ever had the pleasure to encounter. Despite profound disability he has marched along his path of life with vigour, dignity, a sense of humour and an exuberance in life that sometimes takes your breath away!

Go on this journey with Daniel and find a story that is touched with love, grace and realism. It will touch your heart as you accompany him for part of his life – his journey continues with continued hope.

Flo Longhorn
Consultant in Special Education.

Introduction

It was the family chats over the years that prompted me to record some of our experiences together. The recurring question on many of these occasions seemed to be ' do you remember when . . .?' and we would proceed to remind each other, often with great mirth, of some of the situations that centred around Daniel, our younger son who has severe learning difficulties. Following these reminiscences would invariably come the suggestion from my husband, Linbert and elder son, Matthew that I should write them down for posterity. Thus the seed was sown and sprouted to include the other areas of our life together which cannot be separated and which are part of the whole picture.

Let me first set the scene and say a little bit about our family into which Daniel was born. My husband, Linbert was born in Jamaica in 1948 and came to England in 1955 with his parents who had responded to the British Government's invitation to Commonwealth citizens to come and boost the post war depleted workforce. I was born in Buckinghamshire, England in the same year. My parents were Salvation Army Officers (Ministers) and their appointments took them, and consequently me, to a variety of places in England. My formative years were spent in the north of England, moving to London when I was thirteen. Linbert and I met in 1966 at the Salvation Army in Harlesden, North London and married there in 1970. His parents returned to Jamaica in 1971 while mine continued their ministry until their retirement. Linbert's professional background is in community development, having trained at Goldsmith's College, London University. In 1973 he took up an appointment in Scarborough in North Yorkshire, where we spent two years and where in 1974 Matthew was born. A further move took us to Manchester where in 1976 Daniel was born and where we remained for the next twelve years. Linbert has been running his own diversity and equality consultancy firm since 1990 and serves on a number of major public bodies. I was a full time mother but managed to complete an Open University Degree while the boys were still very young. I have since done a number of general courses relating to learning difficulties and most recently completed a postgraduate certificate course in Autism, with Birmingham University.

It would be impossible to summarise anyone's life, particularly a life that is still developing and that is certainly not my intention in this book. What I hope to achieve is to give you, the reader, a glimpse into the everyday life of a family where one member has very special needs. It is simply a sharing of experiences – the joys, traumas, hilarity, embarrassment and exhaustion of life in which Daniel plays a significant role. In spite of the difficulties of coping with Daniel, who often exhibited challenging behaviour, we did what I would call the usual things any family might do. We went shopping, for walks, swimming, to restaurants, on holiday, visiting friends and family and were active members of our church, The Salvation Army, attending Sunday services as well as numerous related activities. Daniel had endless hospital, clinic or doctor's appointments and of course eventually had to go to school. It was a matter of time and experience that taught us how these 'normal' activities presented their own challenges and it is some of these experiences I will share in the following pages. Many of the experiences were humorous, certainly in retrospect, if not at the time and are included because humour has often been our saving grace when we might have felt that we were drowning. These accounts are not intended to degrade Daniel, who has and always will be treated by his family with dignity and respect. What I want to convey is how much we have learned about the importance of accepting each other for who we are rather than for what we do. It is my hope that sharing our story will bring encouragement to others whose lives are challenged in some way.

Chapter 1

WHO IS DANIEL?

As I begin to write this chapter the floor is covered with a mountain of school reports, educational statement, psychologists reports, medical reports and home – school diaries accumulated over the years. Ploughing through the mass of paper I inevitably uncover memories as a young mother of my hopes and dreams for Daniel's progress and experience acute frustration and even some sadness at the immense gap between those hopes for his future and the reality of the present day.

Daniel was born on March 5th 1976 in St Mary's Hospital, Manchester. Apart from some slight blood loss within the first eight weeks my pregnancy and the delivery were normal and Daniel arrived safely weighing seven pounds thirteen ounces. Linbert had been with me at the birth and as we waited to see our new son for the first time I became aware that the medical team seemed to be taking rather a long time to complete the usual post birth procedures. When Daniel had finally been packaged for presentation the doctor, in a very matter of fact way, told us that he had a problem of a cleft palate but that it could be repaired and there was no need to be concerned. He didn't have a hair lip, which usually accompanies a cleft palate, so at least we didn't have the prospect of long-term corrective surgery to add to our concerns. My mind was suddenly in a whirl. In the space of a sentence I had experienced the deep sinking feeling of being told that Daniel had a problem, followed in a breath by an equally deep sense of relief that something could be done about it. When people sometimes casually say "do you want the good news or the bad news first" I think of that doctor. As I held Daniel for the first time and Linbert and I welcomed him to our family he looked so perfect that it was difficult to take in that there was anything wrong at all. Then the doctor pointed out that he also had extra digits on his little fingers but that these would simply be tied and would come away in time. Apparently it was unusual to have extra digits and not extra toes so with a cleft palate but no hair lip Daniel was already establishing himself as out of the ordinary. Little did we know quite how that would manifest itself. Time would, and did, tell.

We listened as the doctor explained that Daniel would have to go into the special care unit as he would need to be tube fed and that a dental plate would eventually be made for him in order to help seal the gaping hole in the roof of his mouth. This would enable him to feed until he was old enough for surgery to be performed to repair his palate. As I began to try and take everything in and cope with the not insignificant ordeal of having just given birth I was given a shot of Pethedin and taken back to the ward to recover. Daniel was taken to the special care unit and Linbert was left to make the usual family phone calls announcing Daniel's birth. I have often thought how difficult and lonely a time that must have been for him but as usual he stoically got on with what had to be done. It must also have been very strange for Matthew who at just two years and two months old had visited me in hospital but had not been allowed to see his new little brother in the special care unit. It was nearly three weeks before the brothers were finally introduced to each other as Daniel had been unable to be discharged until he could satisfactorily feed with the dental plate in his mouth. It was a distressing experience for us to insert this foreign body into his tiny mouth. We could feel his discomfort and wished that he didn't have to endure this procedure. In fact it would be the first of many times when he would have to experience something unpleasant 'for his own good'. After three weeks we were home together as a family at last and life with this 'special' extra person was beginning to take shape. The feeding process was extraordinarily long and increased in time the more Daniel needed to consume for his growth. An eight ounce bottle took at least an hour, sometimes longer, and life seemed to be one long feed. This was difficult for Matthew who by now had begun to realise that this extra person, called his brother, seemed to be taking over. I was very conscious of the need to give Matthew as much time as I could when Daniel was sleeping but it wasn't easy to fit everything in. Life was becoming like the entertainer spinning plates and for me the plate spinning was just beginning.

When Daniel was five months old he was admitted to Pendlebury Childrens' Hospital for surgery to repair his cleft palate. This was going to be a difficult time so my parents took Matthew on holiday for a week in order that Linbert and I could devote our time and energy to being with Daniel. There were very few opportunities in the seventies for parents to stay in hospital with their children so we had to visit at the allotted times which in retrospect seems so clinical yet was accepted because it was the norm. I am horrified now when I think back to that time when Daniel had to spend so much time alone in his hospital cot. Thank goodness for progress. After a week Daniel was discharged along with a pair of arm splints to make sure he didn't put his fingers in his mouth before the stitches healed. His frustration must have been unbearable particularly as he was at the teething stage when a baby's prime occupation is to put his fingers in his mouth. What struck Linbert and I during this time was how placid Daniel was through all this intrusion into his life. In our ignorance we were just grateful that he had coped so well and our hope now was that he would continue to make good progress and that our boys would be able to get to know each other and that some sort of normality would reign, whatever that might mean.

It soon became apparent that although Daniel's motor milestones were on target his mental development was clearly delayed. I had noticed that the sounds he made had an unusual nasal inflection which I assumed was the physical outcome of a shortened palate but he made no usual babbling sounds which would be understood as precursors to speech. He seemed much less alert and attentive than Matthew had been and never raised his arms to signal he wanted lifting up. When I expressed my initial concerns to the doctor he told me that Daniel had much catching up to do after his stressful first few months and that I must try not to compare him with Matthew who had reached all his milestones in record time. I understood what the doctor was saying at the time but I believe there is a difference between comparing the development of children in the sense of marking their progress against each other, and using the information gained from the experience of an older child to help chart the progress of a sibling. I'm sure this is a natural process in any family and I was no different to any mother looking for signs of progress along the developmental pathway. However, there was a marked difference between our boys and time would confirm my instinct that something was far from right in Daniel's development. I continued to monitor his progress and tried hard to take the doctor's advice and give him a chance to catch up. When he was six months old I enrolled myself into a class at the local adult education centre for a couple of hours while Matthew was at nursery school. I registered Daniel into the crèche and informed the staff of his medical history assuring them that he was in good health. I went off to my class feeling that perhaps some sort of normality might be beginning. However, when I went to collect Daniel later that morning the nursery nurse handed him to me, casually saying "he's not normal", and walked away. I was stunned by her insensitivity and wanted to ask her what she had observed in Daniel that caused her to respond in that way but I was too taken aback to find the words. Perhaps she was unable to identify anything in particular but my hurt was compounded by the fact that she had coldly expressed what my instincts had been telling me all along. She may have had reasonable powers of observation but she had much to learn in the area of diplomacy. I never went back to my class.

This experience with the nursery nurse was the first of many that would find me on the receiving end of negative and hurtful comments. I remember being in conversation with some women friends. One of the group was relating a story about a member of her family who had recently given birth to twins and sadly, one of the babies had died. She said how unfair it was that healthy children should be allowed to die while handicapped children are allowed to live. I was stunned by her comment and couldn't believe she could say that, especially in my company, with no thought for my feelings. Did she perceive Daniel as having less right to exist than that baby had? I was too hurt to even find the words to challenge her. When Linbert and I decided to marry we knew we would encounter problems regarding race but we were prepared for that, which was just as well. What we weren't prepared for after Daniel's arrival was the ignorant assumption by some people that Daniel was disabled because he was mixed race. This shocking revelation came when I discovered that a friend had been advised not to get too involved with her 'black boyfriend because they might have a child like Daniel'.

At the age of two years Daniel still showed no sign of speech or pre-speech babble and his noises were different from anything I had ever heard before. He indicated his basic needs by pointing, usually to the cupboard that contained the weetabix and porridge, his favourite foods. He showed little interest in toys, simply turning them round in his hands, and had no imaginative play. Cars or trains were not 'brummed' along the floor, he did not pretend that teddy was having his breakfast, and a large cardboard box was never a garage. With Daniel's medical history still in our minds, Linbert and I were prepared for some developmental delay but had no reason not to expect progress, albeit slowly. However, over time our observations led us to very real concerns about his development and we decided to refer him ourselves to the Child Guidance Clinic where an appointment was made for Daniel to see the psychologist. She gave him a box of toys and watched as he searched through for something that he could hold and turn around neatly in his hands. She then proceeded to show him how to 'brum' the car along the floor and suggested that I spend time at home doing similar things with him. What planet she was on I don't know but I was incensed that she should infer that I hadn't been playing with him and needed to be shown how. I had spent hours with Daniel, often at Matthew's expense, encouraging him to play, trying to include him in Matthew's play, taking him to Mums and Toddlers groups but always he remained distant and disengaged from other people and had little interest in what they were doing.

While I was somewhat aggravated by the attitude of the psychologist the appointment was at least a foot in the door of the long corridor leading to the process of diagnosis which in fact has lasted almost Daniel's lifetime to the present day. At the age of three years he had his first appointment with the neurologist who arranged for an E.E.G. (electro-encephalogram) to be performed to record the electrical activity in the brain in order to determine if any disorder existed. This procedure involves placing electrodes on the scalp, which are then connected to a machine that traces the electrical wave patterns on to graph paper. Daniel was not altogether enamoured with having a head full of what seemed like clothes pegs and having to sit very still but was remarkably controlled and enabled the neurologist to assess that there was some abnormal activity in the speech area. While this information confirmed the obvious, that Daniel had a speech problem, that is he had no speech at all, it didn't tell us why or if anything could or would change. The next step was a brain scan, which was closely followed by a letter from the neurologist saying he was pleased to inform us that Daniel's brain scan was normal. This was a bit like the good news and the bad news yet again. If the scan showed no sign of a problem what did that mean in relation to Daniel's lack of development? We were bewildered and remained in a state of uncertainty desperately wanting some answers to our questions.

In the meantime it was suggested that Daniel attend a nursery unit attached to a school for children who in those days were described as Educationally Sub-normal. The present day designation, having mild to moderate learning difficulties, sounds much kinder. The regime in the nursery was very strict and highly structured to provide a suitable environment for learning to take place but Daniel was completely overpowered by the routine and the behaviour of the children. He became increasingly withdrawn in the situation, crying when work was presented to him and was clearly experiencing a great deal of stress. I will never forget his little sobbing face through the school bus window when, at still only three years old, I sent him off every day to what must have felt to him like a place of torture. I imagined him saying to himself, 'why is mummy doing this to me'? It was a period of deep regret for me. My instinct was to remove him from this daily traumatic experience, yet I convinced myself I had to be cruel to be kind and that it would be for the best in the long term. Apart from that, the professionals had suggested it so it must be right! Fortunately, within the school year, the nursery staff decided that this wasn't the best place for Daniel and I felt vindicated at last. Of course that still left us with the question that has ever since been close to our lips – what next? It was back to the neurologist with a plea for some explanation of Daniel's condition and something we never thought we would hear ourselves saying – 'please give us a label'.

I will never forget how I felt after asking for that information. It appeared that without a medical syndrome a diagnosis could not be made but for the purpose of explaining Daniel's lack of progress and for his future education the only label that could be placed on him was 'mentally handicapped'. The long awaited acknowledgement by the professionals that something was wrong had finally come and was most unwelcome. I went through a bereavement process, experiencing all the stages of grief in one go. I was shocked and numb, confused, hurt and angry. This is what I imagined parents would feel when told at the birth that their child had a disability and we had waited for three years knowing in our minds that something was wrong but hoping in our hearts that somehow Daniel would catch up and our fears would be unfounded. We now had to face reality and the prospect of a future that at that moment seemed overwhelmingly uncertain.

If I thought that 'Educationally Sub-normal' sounded bad then 'Severely Sub-normal' seemed unbearable. I couldn't believe that the previous years of waiting and working with Daniel with the ultimate hope that everything would be fine could end up this way. I had to reassess my thinking and attitudes to disability almost overnight when reality began to set in. I had often had discussions with some of the other women from anti-natal classes how we would feel if we gave birth to a disabled child. Most of them said they wouldn't be able to cope with it and didn't mind if the baby was a boy or girl as long as it was healthy and normal. Strangely enough I never felt able to say that. I didn't think I could live with myself if I gave birth to a child with a disability having previously acknowledged that I wouldn't want to cope with it and would have preferred it to be 'normal'. I always believed that any child was a gift and so tried to prepare myself for any eventuality. When Daniel was born with a cleft palate I guess I thought that was the limit to his disability. During the first three years of uncertainty there was always hope for progress, now I had to put into practice my original conviction that any child was a gift and start the serious business of accepting that Daniel was very special and would need support for the rest of his life. Fortunately, we had no real idea of quite what that would mean for all our lives or we might have been tempted to give up before we had even started, but we knew we had coped so far and committed ourselves to coping with whatever was to come. While we continued to think about the future it soon became apparent that the only way to live was, as the saying goes, 'one day at a time'. It was imperative that each day started positively and that we didn't drag with us the previous day's negative experiences. They belonged to yesterday and if we could we learn from them, we did, if not we had to let them go. This philosophy was much easier to apply when Daniel slept reasonably well and the days were distinguishable by a night in between. As time went by, however, his sleep patterns became increasingly erratic and it was almost impossible to know where one day ended and the next began.

In the early years Daniel was prone to many severe colds and was admitted to Booth Hall Children's Hospital in North Manchester on three separate occasions, in fifteen months, suffering from Pneumonia. Medical investigations concluded that he had an immune globulin deficiency and would need to be treated immediately with antibiotics for any coughs and colds. These three periods in hospital served as Daniel's apprenticeship in how to test the system. This would prove invaluable for the coming years when he was able to put his knowledge to good use. He became adept at drip removal, abseiling down the cot side and absconding at every available opportunity. We very quickly learned to seek medical assistance in the early stages of a cold wishing to avoid hospitalisation at all cost. The placid little baby who had coped so well with his traumatic start to life was beginning to make up for it in no uncertain terms as some of the anecdotal evidence in following chapters will reveal.

Having had no further tests or referrals since the 'mentally handicapped' label had been given, we referred ourselves to the genetics clinic in Manchester when Daniel was seven years old. We were still puzzled about the lack of diagnosis and felt that there must be something that we could find out about his condition as well as perhaps eliminating the uncertainty of any inherited condition that might affect Matthew's future children. A skin biopsy was taken from Daniel to test for chromosome abnormality while Linbert, Matthew and myself were given blood tests. All the results proved negative and we were at least somewhat assured that Daniel was a 'one-off'- as if we didn't already know this! We remained in a state of unknowing for the next four years, simply trying to manage his increasingly extreme behaviour, until we moved to Bedford where, in 1987, at a Child Development Centre Clinic, we met Dr Ricks from the Department of Paediatrics, University College London. He was a very gracious gentleman, most generous in his acknowledgment of our efforts as parents, never once suggesting that we could have done anything more to help Daniel. In the clinic the doctor observed Daniel's unremitting activity of grabbing peoples' clothing, upturning everything on his desk, throwing toys around the room whilst judging the effect of his actions and weighing up the possible reprimand. He succinctly described his behaviour as 'constant guerrilla warfare'. The doctor also witnessed what he described as the hair trigger quality of Daniel's responses. When thwarted he erupted very quickly into an agitated state, biting his hands, banging his head and slapping his face. When I mentioned his erratic sleep pattern it appeared that the speed with which he fell asleep and woke up also reflected this hair trigger quality. Daniel never gave himself time to wake up. There was no stretching or becoming acclimatised to the day, it was almost as if the night had never been. In spite of the absence of any particular obsessional behaviour at this stage, Dr Ricks concluded that Daniel had 'the wary, impaired quality of an autistic child' and had sufficient features to justify his being considered for a placement that would take these autistic features into account. At long last someone had given us a label. Of course we knew that nothing would dramatically change but we could learn about the condition and at least try and explain, if only to ourselves, why he behaved in certain ways and if there were things that we could put in place to make his world less confusing. His behaviour would always challenge simply because the nature of autism meant that he would not be able to take into account, in any meaningful way, the implications of his actions on other people. The Doctor's report could hardly have been completed when the missing obsessional behaviour appeared. It wasn't that it hadn't existed but rather that we hadn't recognised it as such as it wasn't as extreme as we were to subsequently experience. Three main obsessions of 'kite making', 'drinking' and 'waving' emerged over different periods of time and remain very much a part of Daniel's life now and as such require some elaboration in order to convey a clear picture of who he is.

Early photographs remind us that from about the age of two years Daniel always carried a stick-like object in his hands. Over the years he has developed an extensive range from garden twigs, coat hangers, wooden spoons, dish mops, spatulas to fly swatters. This interest took on an added impetus following a visit to Dunstable Downs when we first moved to Bedfordshire in 1986. Daniel was fascinated by the kites the children were flying so big brother, Matthew, enterprising as ever, found a piece of string which he tied to the end of his stick referring to it as 'your kite'. Little did Matthew know that this simple act of brotherly love would turn into one of the most enduring 'hobbies' of his little brother. Daniel was thrilled with the innovation and from then on insisted that his variety of sticks be referred to as kites. Incidentally, when you have no speech by which to communicate your preferred designation you simply stick the stick or rather 'kite' into someone's face until they use the correct terminology. They soon learn. Daniel continued to develop his hobby, as we like to call it, adorning his kites with all sorts of bits and pieces such as sticky sweets, plastercine, play dough, sellotape, and the ultimate, for by far the longest period of time, an assortment of elastic bands which he used either to hold other things in place or simply as embellishments in their own right. The elastic bands became central to the completion of a kite and his eagle eye would spot one at a hundred metres. We couldn't get out of a shop without a bag of elastics and our local post office and post lady used to save their spares especially for Daniel. It became a regular social occasion to go to the shop specifically for elastic bands and Daniel, knowing exactly where they were located, would stride purposefully towards

Daniel with one of his first coathanger 'kites' – sharing a chair with cousin Caroline and brother Matthew.

them then queue very impatiently with me to pay for them. He could never quite see the point in that part of the exercise. The elastics have taken more of a back seat recently but the kite collection continues and has progressed to stones or palm sized objects, which he constantly turns around in his hands. Daniel's kites are always quality tested for strength across his knees. Those that snap are ungraciously abandoned and the search quickly begins for another. He will strip all the unwanted knotty bits of bark with his teeth transferring the debris to his face, which then resembles the dirty twig he has now transformed into a beautifully smooth piece of wood. Once he is satisfied with his completed work of art and it has outlived its purpose he will loft it, often deliberately into the neighbour's garden, to rest in peace. He has been quite bemused when our patient neighbour has, from time to time, returned a bag full of kites for re-use.

Stripping a twig ready for 'kite' duty.

As parents we were advised by the educational psychologist to try and re-direct Daniel's obsession on the basis that he became distressed and agitated when parted from his kites and this prevented him from focussing on a given task intended to aid his development. We were, and still are aware of the negative aspects of Daniel's hobby. He is totally driven to finding suitable kite material and will behave like a man possessed searching for and destroying things to get or produce what he needs. When kites don't cooperate, that is when sticks break or he can't find the right size or shape then he becomes very distressed and difficult to manage. The positive aspects of his kite making, however, mean that he is focussed, often quite calm and able to concentrate on what he is doing for considerable periods of time. He uses initiative and discrimination in his search for materials and it is surely a creative expression of something within himself although not necessarily obvious to anyone else – particularly when he has destroyed their possessions. No-one has yet suggested where or to what we redirect this obsession and it remains a point of concern to us that connections are rarely made between so-called abnormal and normal behaviours. People can pollute the air with cigarette smoke, roll out of pubs in a state of inebriation, spend hours on the golf course or in the gym, collect stamps, in fact indulge in almost any obsession in the name of leisure and it is not challenged. I feel that obsessions should not simply be seen as negative distractions but that the positive elements of hard work and creativity should be recognised and valued.

It is difficult to remember quite when drinking became an obsession. From his early childhood Daniel would only ever drink tea, never fruit juice or the typical fizzy drinks that children would usually kill for. It was only when we went on holiday to Jamaica in 1987 that he allowed himself to experience the delights of ice cold drinks, probably out of desperation in the extreme heat. It wasn't a significant turning point, however, because on our return to England it was back to the good old cup of tea again. It was about this time that he was put on a variety of medications to either calm him down or help him sleep and I think this was the start of the slippery slope. While he may have at times experienced genuine thirst I think that was the precursor to what has become a real obsession. Daniel will drink incessantly if given the chance and if not he will steel anyone's cup of anything. If a cup is placed down on a table for a second it will vanish before the owner's eyes and if the person is not looking he will question his sanity and probably convince himself that he was dreaming he had a drink. The after service cup of tea or coffee at Church is his idea of heaven on earth – or at church – as he darts from table to table whisking full cups, half cups or just the dregs, anything will do. He is as driven to obtain a drink as he is to find a new kite and he will go to any lengths to achieve his aim. Apart from our concern over health and hygiene issues Daniel also puts himself at risk of scalding either by attempting to pour from a boiling kettle or by grabbing hot drinks from peoples hands. Although we never gave him coffee, and as far as we know none of his carers have done so either, he has developed a real passion for it. This resulted in him suffering a major caffeine overdose when he secretly made himself a drink consisting of a cup full of neat coffee and about half an inch of water. Not even his constitution could take this and he slumped to the floor smashing his two front teeth in the process. He spent the night in hospital in a very distressed state but things could have been so much worse. He apparently hasn't learned from this experience as he has recently been caught red-handed doing the exact same thing. This is certainly not an innocuous habit and if the professionals could come up with any suggestions for this we would all be very grateful.

Finally 'waving'. This must have started when he learned to wave goodbye and while it may seem to be the least of the problems it can be one of the most annoying and exhausting. Daniel has to wave at everyone and everything, what seems like a hundred times, before he can move on. Before leaving the house he waves at everyone left in it, the bird, the dining table, the piano, the kettle, the chairs, everything in fact that exists and finally has to be hauled out by almost any means to break the cycle which he is unable to break for himself. Once outside he waves at the car on the driveway and every other stationary vehicle he passes, standing to observe each one before finally moving further along the road. In his more mischievous moments he will try a car door handle to initiate a response from me, or perhaps it is in the hope of a lift! The manager of a day centre that Daniel attends bravely took him on a trip to London and experienced his three obsessions at first hand. He was on constant vigil for new kites through the busy London streets, found a discarded drinks can on the ground which he drained of its' dregs and insisted on waving goodbye to everyone and everything in the underground train as Jane desperately tried to get him out before the doors closed. I have such admiration for carers who are brave enough to risk such experiences. My years with Daniel leave me saying 'not likely' or 'never again'. There isn't much more to be said about waving except that you can only wave goodbye for so long before wanting to scream 'just go away'.

Daniel was described as having autistic features, so what does that actually mean? Autistic Spectrum Disorder is a complex neurological disability with no known cause. The word spectrum is used because the condition includes a range of developmental differences.

However, everyone with autism will have an impairment of social interaction, communication and imagination. This is referred to as the triad of impairments[1]. For instance, a problem with social interaction might show in a person's difficulty with social relationships, appearing to be aloof or indifferent. A problem with social communication may be revealed by difficulties with verbal and non-verbal communication, for example not understanding the meaning of gestures, facial expressions or tone of voice. There may also be a tendency to understand language very literally – for example a simple request to 'give me your hand', when crossing a road could cause utter confusion. A person with autism may be unable to play imaginatively, focussing on an object, such as an earring, rather than the person wearing it, or a piece of a toy rather than the whole thing. They may copy or repeat activities but are unable to initiate through imagination and they often pursue activities rigidly and repetitively – sometimes obsessively. Daniel meets all these criteria and as such fits on the spectrum. However, autism can also be present alongside other disabilities and it was interesting to have a further insight into his disability when in 2000 Heidi, his house parent from his Camphill Community in Scotland, read in a medical journal an article about Smith-Magenis Syndrome[2]. Heidi felt that Daniel had many of the characteristics appertaining to this condition and sent us a copy of the article for our opinion. We couldn't believe that something could describe him so accurately. The list included self-injury, sleep disturbance, developmental delay, an underdeveloped (flat) face, chronic ear infections, short fingers and toes, an unusual gait, decreased sensitivity to pain, difficulty in chewing, hyperactivity and destructive behaviour. Apparently children with Smith-Magenis syndrome are born with a small deletion of one member of their 17th pair of chromosomes and it is the lack of this specific section known as –17 that causes the child to develop the features of the syndrome. There was only one way to find out if Heidi's and our feelings were right and that meant a referral to the Genetics Department of Grampian University Hospital. The blood test did indeed show a deletion of part of one chromosome 17 and confirmed that Daniel had Smith-Magenis Syndrome. The syndrome is rare although it is thought that the true incidence is higher than is classified. This is not surprising as it was only through the chance reading (or was it chance?) of the article by Heidi that we were able to pursue a diagnosis for Daniel and I guess there may be many more parents who, like us, have never come across it before. Sometimes discoveries seem to be very arbitrary and one wonders how many people slip the net and miss out on vital information and support.

Hopefully, this chapter will have set the scene for the following pages, which describe, through real life experiences, who Daniel really is and which will fill in the gaps that make up life.

Chapter 2

AND SO TO SCHOOL

There has been some justifiable criticism in recent years of the frequent changes of designation in the field of disability. However, I believe that one of the significant positive changes has been from the term 'severely subnormal' to 'severe learning difficulties'. The word 'subnormal' has connotations of 'sub-standard' or 'second class' and when attached to 'child' or 'adult' has implications for the person to whom it is applied. Daniel was not subnormal, substandard or second class, he was a child who had difficulties in certain areas of life. Unfortunately, at the time of his admission to school, the former term was in use and I feel contributed to the stigma attached to mental disability. I had never heard the term physical sub-normality and couldn't see why mental disability should be described in this way. It all added to the burden of accepting that Daniel did have acute difficulties and life would not be easy for any of us. It was with very mixed feelings therefore that we took him to Leacroft School in North Manchester in 1980. In many ways it felt like a retrograde step as we had so hoped that he would have caught up by now but of course we knew that he was going to need specialist teaching and had to accept that from now on this would be the educational environment for Daniel.

I was amazed at the sense of peace I experienced on that first day. The atmosphere was calm and welcoming, the children were happy and the teachers were understanding and very caring. I came home feeling that at last Daniel was in the right place and if it was right for him then it was right for us also. He spent a very happy year at Leacroft and I also benefited from some of the training courses on offer, from behaviour modification programmes initiated by Manchester University Education Department to the most significant in terms of Daniel's progress, the then very new Makaton sign system, devised by Margaret Walker and based on a simplified version of British Sign Language. This opened up a whole new world of communication for him. He devoured new signs and although the idea is to work systematically through the stages in the manual we soon found ourselves breaking the rules to accommodate his desire for signs to represent his interests. It was an exciting time and good to feel that we could lessen his frustration at having no verbal communication. Leacroft School and in particular Head teacher Joan Boucher provided much needed support in those early days of schooling and were instrumental in helping us as parents to adjust to the reality of our situation.

A house move to South Manchester meant a new school for Daniel and so in Autumn 1981 he made his presence felt at The Birches where for the next five years we were all supported by caring and competent staff who continued the good work which had commenced at Leacroft. During this time Linbert was offered a job in London, which he accepted. I was not happy to lose the support systems that we had in Manchester which included family and friends as well as excellent education and medical provision so it was decided that Linbert would stay in London during the week and come home at weekends. We survived this way of life for fifteen months, unsuccessfully trying to pack being a family into two very short days of the weekend, until we came to the obvious conclusion that a move would have to take place. I didn't want to live in London even if we had been able to afford to, so the question was how close could we get to make commuting reasonable and a house affordable, not to mention the provision of a special school and support services for Daniel. I wanted to have good access to Manchester so limited the search for a home to north of London writing to Hertfordshire, Buckinghamshire and Bedfordshire for information on special schools and associated provision. The only information I received came from Bedford and so the decision was taken to set up home there. While we were house hunting we made an appointment to visit St. John's School where we met the formidable Head teacher Flo Longhorn for the first time. Her reputation had gone before her and she lived up to it in every way. She epitomised optimism, generosity and a positive spirit and this extension of her personality was apparent throughout the school. I felt particularly ill at ease with the prospect of this major move but meeting Flo helped me to believe that this might just work out for Daniel's good and when she agreed to take him into school it somehow confirmed the 'rightness' of it. In June 1986 when Matthew was twelve and Daniel ten years old it had all happened and we were now living in Bedfordshire. Yet again we were privileged to be on the receiving end of excellent teaching and care often above and beyond the call of duty. The friendship and support of Head teacher Flo, Deputy head teacher Christine and all the staff at the school saw us through some very difficult times of transition, the most significant of these being Daniel's move after four years at St. John's to a residential placement. It had become apparent that Daniel would not cope well with the transition to the further education department of the school. The emphasis there was on preparation for adulthood and possibly a more independent life outside of school when the time came. It was a period for the students when the structures would gradually be reduced and it was clear that Daniel, although only thirteen years old at the time, was going to need a much more structured approach and in fact a twenty four hour curriculum.

The suggestion that his needs would be best met in a residential situation came unexpectedly and although Linbert and I had discussed the possibility and even the inevitability of a residential placement at some time we hadn't anticipated the reality of it quite so soon. I don't know if I could ever have made the decision myself to let him go even though life with him was utterly exhausting. I could only commit to the idea once the educational psychologist persuaded me it was in Daniel's best interest and wasn't being suggested because I couldn't cope any more. Once again the maternal instinct to do one's best for one's child took over and the process of looking for yet another right place began. Flo gave us a mound of literature relating to possible places to visit and after listing all the requirements we felt would be essential for Daniel's well being and development we soon eliminated most of them except for one brochure which leapt out from all the others and contained details of the Camphill Schools and Communities. This was to be the entry into a whole new world for all of us.

The Camphill Experience

As I read through the literature about the Camphill communities[3] generally and the schools in particularly I was struck by the philosophy on which it was all based. I had only vaguely heard of Rudolf Steiner and knew nothing of his philosophical works so it was with interest that I read how his philosophy of acceptance of the spiritual uniqueness of each human being was applied to community living. The Camphill Movement, founded in 1940, comprises therapeutic communities, which include people with learning disabilities, where everyone can live and work with others and develop relationships based on mutual care and respect. The emphasis is on the creation of communities *with* people who have special needs rather than *for* them and as such are a true expression of inclusion and acceptance. A further scan through the literature gave me a glimpse of the wonderful cultural life and the special seasonal celebrations experienced by the members and gave me a real sense that this would be a wonderful environment for Daniel to live in. A visit to the Camphill School in Aberdeen confirmed for us that it would be right for

34

Daniel and we were simultaneously relieved and apprehensive that they agreed to take him. It was difficult to reconcile the feelings of relief and apprehension. As always, when trying to do the best for Daniel we had mixed feelings. On this occasion we knew we would experience some relief from the constant burden of care but the thought of him having to leave home at all, let alone to be over five hundred miles away was difficult to come to terms with. Life can be a real paradox.

Nothing could have prepared me for how I would feel the day we took him to his new school. We travelled on the sleeper and Daniel was quite bemused at the idea of sleeping in a bed on a train. He eventually fell asleep but my mind was in turmoil wondering how we were going to explain what was happening to him, that we weren't abandoning him and would see him soon. How could we possibly prepare him. He had such limited conceptual ability and would not be able to understand why this was happening or when he would ever see us again. Tomorrow, next week or next month would be completely meaningless to him. We arrived in Aberdeen at about 7.30 in the morning and had breakfast in the hotel opposite the station. I could hardly eat while Daniel innocently wolfed down a full Scottish breakfast. Bernhard and Kerry were to be Daniel's house-parents and had already suggested that we didn't prolong the agony by staying too long so our return journey was booked for mid-day. We helped to settle Daniel in and unpack his bags but it was soon time to leave for the station. There are no words to describe how I felt as I hugged him goodbye and was led to the car unable to see through my streaming tears. Never was a journey so long or a house so empty when we returned home without him. The sleepless nights and exhausting days sank into insignificance as I sank into despair wondering yet again – have we made the right decision, what is Daniel thinking, how is he feeling, will he be well cared for? We all experienced much pain at this time but it is impossible to estimate how Matthew must have felt through it all. Although having been subject to many of Daniel's misdemeanours and so often having had to take second place in terms of our time with him, he still had a strong bond with his little brother even if he did want to kill him at times.

Brothers in 'conversation'.

Looking at photographs.

They say time is a great healer but it is also often the only measure of whether a decision is right or not. It wasn't long before we knew our agony had been worth it. Daniel soon became part of the extended family of St Andrews house on Murtle Estate in the beautiful setting beside the River Dee in Bieldside on the outskirts of Aberdeen. The holistic approach adopted by Camphill ensures a balanced and integrated life for everyone in the community. Within a house there are pupils of all ages and abilities, house-parents who are responsible for the overall running of the house, co-workers who would look after two or three young people plus teachers and therapists who would also be resident. There is real continuity of care, which is of particular importance to the well being of those with a disability. Daniel was able to benefit from this personally as well as experience the many varied cultural activities, especially the celebration of Christian festivals throughout the year. It would be impossible to relate or evaluate all Daniel's experiences during his school time in Camphill but we know that we had more than sufficient confidence in this way of life to want it to continue. The time was fast approaching when Daniel would have to move on to a further education placement and, feeling no need to look beyond Camphill for this, we looked at communities in Wales, Yorkshire and finally Stonehaven just south of Aberdeen. It was about this time that we started to sense the shift of priorities in our local authority. Just three years earlier we were told it would be in Daniel's best interest to be placed residentially. Now as the policy of 'care in the community' was beginning to take effect there was a distinct feeling that from now on we might have to fight for Daniel's placement but so far so good. It was eventually agreed that after completing his schooling in Aberdeen in July 1993 he would make the transition to Templehill Community near Stonehaven after the summer holiday and so another chapter of his life began.

Heidi and Michael were to be Daniel's house-parents for the next seven years and as our knowledge of them grew over this time so did our respect and appreciation for who they were and what they did for Daniel and everyone else who came under their influence. For the next seven years we visited at least twice a year for Daniel's birthday and parents weekend and on all these occasions, through our observations and discussions as well as being part of the family for a while, we learned much about the Camphill way and how it impacted the daily lives of those sharing in it. The literature that had convinced us to pursue this as an option for Daniel in the first place was quite accurate. It described the life of any Camphill Community as revolving around the essential work of keeping the community functioning and encouraging each member to contribute, according to their ability, to the well being of each other. We were able to witness the working out of this philosophy where each individual played a part in the whole process of an activity. The everyday activity of bread making, for instance, involved those who baked it, those who collected it from the bakery and delivered it to the individual houses, those who set it on the table, those who cleared the table and of course everyone who consumed it. In a similar way, the activity of gardening had many individual components from digging, preparing the soil, planting, weeding, maintaining, harvesting, delivery to the houses, food preparation in the kitchen, cooking, eating and clearing away. All the individual jobs would be given equal importance and those involved would be helped to understand their relationship to the whole as well as having value in their own right. Daniel's part in this process began in the garden with the job of raking up, piling the debris into a wheelbarrow and taking it to the compost heap. This process involved many skills such as coordination, balance, following instructions and cooperation with others to name but a few. Anyone who has attempted to wheel a barrow, which usually has a mind of its own, aught to appreciate the skill in this manoeuvre. We felt that this was quite an accomplishment for Daniel so we bought him his own wheelbarrow and had his name emblazoned along the side of it. He seemed quite impressed but I don't think it inspired him to work any harder. Over the years Daniel has participated in many craft workshops such as basket making, weaving, pottery, candle making and woodwork as well as the gardening, log cutting and feeding the goats and chickens. He loved the weekly folk dancing, the importance of which should not be underestimated as, unlike disco, it had a structured form requiring cooperation with a partner and the need to follow instructions. As Daniel had no obvious desire to either cooperate or be instructed it became an important and challenging learning situation for him. Art and music therapy were an important part of his curriculum and attendance at musical concerts added greatly to his quality of life. Last but by no means least were the regular long walks in the beautiful Scottish countryside and special outdoor pursuits weeks during the year.

Daniel spent nearly eleven years in Camphill in Scotland but as they say 'all good things must come to an end'. At twenty four years old he was now too old for a further education placement and required a fifty two week adult placement. This, combined with the current policy of the local authority that anyone placed out of county should be found a place locally, meant that he had to leave Scotland returning to Bedfordshire in November 2000. I felt almost as distraught at him leaving Camphill as I had felt when I left him there in January 1990 believing then, and since confirming, that nothing could match it. I will share some of Daniel's 'adult' experiences in my conclusions to the book but will conclude this chapter with some of the comments taken directly from his school reports and home–school diaries over the years and they really say it all. We have laughed so much as we have read some of these reports but often the humour is tinged with some sadness at the seeming lack of progress, as my bracketed comments will show. We are still more than a little frustrated that so often Daniel's behaviour is typical of autistic spectrum disorder which these days would probably have been diagnosed. This is not to say that his development would necessarily have been very different or that those working with him, including ourselves, would have had any less expectations of him. However, a knowledge of autism would have at least helped us to understand that certain areas of life would be confusing and uncomfortable if not very difficult for him.

Selected extracts from school reports:-

Leacroft
1980 – Daniel plays by himself a lot.

1981 – Daniel attempts to use educational toys but quickly loses interest and turns the pieces round in his hands. He likes to feel objects and textures. He prefers to feel the sand in the tray rather than use a bucket and spade.

The Birches
1982 – Daniel is easily distracted by noise. He also prefers to investigate in a tactile way – usually in the middle of a task. He accepts the attention of other children for a short while then he becomes very irritated.

1983 – It has always been difficult to find something that would motivate him to work. We have to take care that the materials with which he is working are not too interesting to feel. He can collect his own coat and be sent for another child's coat – he recognises them all.
We are using signs for 'now' and 'later' in an effort to stop Daniel from asking repeated questions.
He constantly asks us to sign the same thing over and over again. (He still does in 2003)
He is still more rewarded by doing something wrong than doing it correctly and any mistake must therefore be ignored completely. (Easier said than done – especially when presented with a handful of faeces)

1984 – He has stopped undoing his shoelaces all the time. (This didn't last – he still does it today)
1985 – A well-structured environment is helpful as Daniel responds well to routine. (Still applies)

St. Johns
1986 – Daniel tackles several construction tasks, although he appears to prefer to disassemble the pieces rather than assemble them. (Couldn't be more true)

Camphill School
1990 – Daniel is always eager to bid a fond farewell – refusing to go out until he has waved goodbye individually to everyone around him. (He's not drowning – he's waving). This behaviour is characteristic of Daniel as a whole – that he is ever eager to rush on to the next event or linger in the past and is rarely able to live in the present.

1991 – Daniel enjoys folk dancing and now accepts with good grace that he must move at the same time as his partner.

1992 – Daniel is a warm, friendly, lively youngster but he has some very anti-social ways of getting the attention he seeks. (Nicely understated) In order to help him mature, he needs a secure environment with a predictable and meaningful rhythm and routine.

1993 – Movement exercises - Daniel has great difficulty in walking forward or backward without swaying strongly from side to side. (His sways are considerably wider and stronger in 2003)

Pottery - Daniel was very keen to do pottery and with the aid of plaster moulds was able to make some very acceptable dishes and bowls. If not watched closely, however, he had a tendency to ruin his work but was clearly not happy once having done it.

Behaviour - Daniel is still very dependent upon the adult who he is used to supporting him. A newcomer will experience his most questionable behaviour in all its full glory.

Domestic tasks - Daniel does not enjoy involving himself in daily duties which he considers rather beneath his dignity and he will shirk any job given the chance. (Who wouldn't)

Templehill Community

1994 – Daniel is always in motion, even when standing in one place or sitting on a chair usually with sticks or stick-like objects in his hands. The need to obtain suitable kites is a daily necessity, although a stick may be replaced by a coat hanger, wooden spoon, cheese slicer or any other kitchen utensil of suitable size. He likes to decorate the ends of his objects with an elastic band, even going to the extreme of climbing out of the window of his room (ground floor) in the middle of the night in order to collect one he had seen in one of the other houses. If an elastic band is not available he is prepared to use elastic from a sock or torn from rubber gloves. Daniel needs the constant awareness of a co-worker but also appreciates times when he can be allowed to sit in his room in peace.

1995 – Daniel's motivation is not strong when it comes to a work situation. In basket and woodwork he was a more interested observer of others' work than his own.

1996 – Daniel's undiminished interest centres round his sticks. Not every stick is good enough and he will carefully select the right one, break it into the right length and bite off the bark if necessary. At other times a wooden spoon is chosen or straightened-out headphones will be used. In this respect Daniel has no sense of value. Objects are judged by their suitability for his purpose and he inexorably and determinedly sets out to find them.

Daniel's work on the estate involves going to the croft each morning to feed the goats – this was much appreciated by him as the road follows the shelter belt with an inexhaustible supply of twigs and sticks. In recent months Daniel has started to wander off the estate. It is difficult to know where he would be going as he always appears to be on the search for sticks. He therefore needs constant supervision. It remains a concern that without it only his obsessions supply any motivation for activity.

1997 – This has become a stone year. Sticks have become less and less interesting to him. He used all opportunities to climb out of his bedroom window as the surrounding area was littered with enticing stones. Daniel needs to find a strength in himself to establish a balance in his patterns of behaviour. Unless he is supervised at all times there is no knowing what he will do next. He finds peace and rest when in the vicinity of an adult who seems to provide a 'backbone' for him.

1998 - Although Daniel's general behaviour has improved there are still many moments when he will fall back into his old ways as soon as he is left by himself, such as on the toilet – with subsequent smearing. It remains a concern that in spite of his age (now 22) he continues to need one to one supervision day and night. When meeting him one always thinks 'if only he would, because one feels that he could'.

Daniel's favourite activities are unchanged: - folk dancing, swimming and listening to music, especially live concerts. He also enjoys garden and estate work, especially wheel-barrowing.

1999 – Daniel can be very sociable, seeking the company of others (on his own terms of course). He has a sense of fun and can burst into fits of laughter particularly when he observes someone else being naughty.

Woodwork – He has learned to rasp a lamp base out of a log but he does not like sand - papering as he sees no purpose in it. His integration in the group is only fleeting. Most of the time he ignores others and is absorbed in rocking with his sticks or stones when not working.

Basketwork – Daniel's project has been waste paper baskets with straight sides and he has made five or six in the course of the year. He is very proud of these baskets and has enjoyed giving some away and taking some home as presents.

Daniel is beginning to show that he is outgrowing the provision that we can offer here and that he needs a more permanent fifty two week placement. The coming year will be his last at Templehill and we look forward to preparing him for another step in his development.

2000 – Daniel depends on a structured environment where a certain amount of behaviour modification is expected. A firm approach helps him to find the boundaries which he does not seem able to set for himself. Too many changes in staff would cause insecurity. He has shown that he needs continuous support, help and supervision and if given this can contribute to a social set up with his genuine interest, warmth and care for people around him.

Selected extracts from home – school diaries

Home – 7th April. If Daniel looks a bit bald on the left side it's because he gave himself a short back and sides.

Home – 15th April. He's done it again. Scissors are now permanently banned.

School – 15th April. Daniel is truly amazing. I can't take my eyes off him for a minute.

School – 30th April. It has been several days since Daniel undid his shoelaces. He is teasing the new nursery nurse and it's interesting to observe his reactions to things asked of him. He bites his hand, squeals and then looks utterly fed up when she persists.

School – 28th June. Daniel has had a yo-yo week. He was very disruptive at the beginning of the week, pushing, taking children's toys etc – but improved as the week progressed.

Home – 2nd July. Daniel was also disruptive at home. Toileting was very haphazard – twice emptying 'poo'. It's very difficult to watch him for a whole day – can't wait for the holidays – what joy!

School – 4th July. We are spending Friday at the park. Would you send a sun hat for Daniel in case of hot weather.
Home – 5th July. Sorry, I have no hat for Daniel. I abandoned them when he was three as he threw them all away.

Home – 24th July. Another emptied nappy!

School – 25th July. Daniel handed the dinner lady a handful of 'poo' today. She was not amused.

School – 1st October. We had a super game of snap today – matching numbers 1,2 and 3. Enclosed the cards for you to have a go at home.

Home – 2nd October. Daniel would have nothing to do with the cards. When I called him over to do them he took them and threw them up the passage. He seems to think school work belongs in school, not at home and never the twain shall mix!

Home – 7th October. Daniel has a sore finger. I've tried keeping a plaster on it but without success. He is leaving the house wearing one and is under threat to keep it on in school but he has a very short memory and it will probably be off before the bus turns the corner. The problem is, I know what the results of these minor ailments can be for Daniel – numerous visits to outpatients. Horrors.

School – 7th October. Put new plasters on three times then gave up.

Home – 16th October. He had pinched my new bra and shredded it in his bedroom, then had a smashing time with the eggs from the fridge. Found them scrambled on the worktop. Great way to start the day.

Home – 18th October. Another empty nappy this morning!

School – 4th November. Sorry about the torn trousers. He was supposed to be watching T.V.

School – 6th February. I got so cross with Daniel yesterday that he got no dinner. He took his hearing aid apart, broke a toy and undid his shoelaces several times on the bus back from swimming. He has been a saint today.

School – 10th February. I'm telling Daniel that if he takes his laces out in the minibus there will be no swimming. Will you please remind him on Monday morning?

Home – 13th February. Have warned him about his laces but he seems to have changed his tactics over the weekend and is taking his trousers down instead. Ever feel you are fighting a losing battle?

I guess many of us looking back at our old school reports will read phrases such as 'could do better', 'has great potential', 'lacks motivation' and so forth. While the words may not sound so different from some of those on Daniel's reports there is a significant difference in their potential effectiveness for change. We who do not have a particular neurological dysfunction have a choice about what we do on reading such comments about ourselves. Even if we have a family history of low academic achievement and have no expectation that we will be able to change the mould, we have the mental capacity to imagine how things could change and have the ability to consider what would motivate us to do better. Motivation comes from knowing or understanding the reason for doing or not doing something. Daniel and others like him, particularly those on the autistic spectrum, do not possess this level of understanding and therefore often cannot see the point of an activity or why something should be considered 'naughty'. Knowing that he will be in trouble for ripping his clothes beyond recognition is not sufficient to prevent Daniel from doing it. Whether the thought of any consequence ever crosses his mind or if he just takes a calculated risk that his action is worth the retribution I don't know, but he rarely shows concern about the effect of his behaviour – which is usually to cause me to rant and rave. Perhaps the anticipation of my response is his motivation, although I have to say in my own defence that most of the time I am reasonably calm in my response in order not to give him the satisfaction of seeing me jump up and down. However, the quality of my response seems to make little difference to his future behaviour. I have heard people say that he knows what is right and wrong but in actual fact he only knows that someone has said that something is wrong. He doesn't have an innate sense of right and wrong which might prompt him to consider the effect of his actions on others. In this respect he fits classically on the autistic spectrum in that he is unable to put himself in the position of another. While he may learn that a particular action is unacceptable he will not have any real appreciation of the reason why. We moderate our behaviour because we have an awareness and appreciation of the implications of our actions on other people. Without that awareness there is no apparent need to change what we do. Social graces are only relevant if social acceptance is desired. With no real understanding of this concept there can be no understanding of the need to adjust one's behaviour.

On looking back over Daniel's school reports and exchanges between home and school I can't help feeling that an awareness that he had this conceptual difficulty may have altered the approach to his learning. If we as parents, as well as the teachers who worked with him, had understood that he didn't necessarily deliberately set out to cause the extreme annoyance which followed so many of his actions but that he actually didn't have the mental capacity to 'care' then perhaps our approach may have been different. One would hope that at least our reactions may have been slightly less explosive and that we may have reduced our frustration a little. If only I knew then what I know now, but I didn't and all I can do now is continue to pass on such accumulated knowledge that I have to those who are helping Daniel in his adult life. I conclude this chapter with some selected words addressed personally to Daniel by his teachers in the Camphill School in Scotland. They are very special to me as they express something of the real essence of who Daniel is and that he is special in his own right.

1990
Dear Daniel

This is your first year in the class and there are many new things aren't there? It is good that you are so lively and full of fun, Daniel. You are always in movement, like a river rushing down over rocks, splashing and bubbling. From the high mountains where the light sparkles, your river runs and races. I hope that one day soon we can channel your bubbling brook into a quiet pool where it can flow strongly and slowly. Your shining eyes tell us that you enjoy listening to stories and music. I am glad that you can sit and listen well now and are learning to be peaceful. Soon I am sure you will be eager to work hard and learn all about the world.

Chris.

1991

Dear Daniel

You have now spent more than a year in our class and have made many friends. You have become a good listener although you have still not lost your wonderful humour! Do you remember all the subjects we learned together? I am sure you will not forget the fiery volcanoes that we made.

Now Daniel, you will go to a new class. We will miss you but hope that you will make many new steps. I hope you will be at peace in your new class. It is very good to have quiet moments. Every lively, crackling fire has to come to rest and give us a calm, warm glow! I wish you well on your new journey Daniel.

Chris.

1992

Dear Daniel

Now you have been in this class for a year. You have brought so much warmth and fun with you that it is hard to remember the mischief which also came. You are beginning to learn that you cannot always do what you like. In the coming year you must learn to like what you do.

Do you remember looking at Greek art and seeing how much care those artists put into their work? Now you are sixteen you must learn to care about what you do.

I look forward to welcoming you back to class and accompanying you a little further towards adulthood.

Paul.

Chapter 3

ON THE HOME FRONT

When a new baby arrives into a family it is often said 'life will never be the same again'. Never was a truer word said than after the arrival of Daniel into our family. Apart from the endless round of hospital or doctor's appointments there were the everyday things to be done. Everyone had to eat and sleep, the house had to be cleaned, the garden maintained, shopping had to be done, pets needed caring for, appointments had to be kept, school, church and social life all had to be synchronised. For a busy family this balance is usually a work of art, for a busy family with Daniel in it, it had the potential at best to be less than finely tuned or at worst, completely discordant. One thing could be guaranteed however, and that was that life was neither boring nor predictable. I guess those two words often go together and usually have negative connotations but there were times when boring and predictable would have been very welcome.

Quality Controller.
In the kitchen Daniel was known as the quality controller as he always had his fingers in everything dipping and

testing just to make sure it all met with his approval. He was completely fascinated by the food preparation process and just had to be involved, on his own terms of course. He chopped vegetables with a vengeance whether I wanted them or not. He was an ace with a tin opener and often I would find my stock of tins of beans or spaghetti lined up like soldiers with raised caps taking the salute on the kitchen worktop. One Christmas I had dutifully sweat over a hot stove to make what seemed like an endless batch of mince pies for the post Carol Service refreshments, only to find that during the cooling process a little finger had been poked through the top of every one of my creations. I always knew there must be a good use for glace cherries. They gave the mince pies that extra seasonal look. Daniel's eating habits left a lot to be desired and even now after years of teaching, prompting and reminding how to use a knife and fork and keep his food in his mouth it is still advisable for those in the vicinity to wear a mackintosh and galoshes. While he was living in the Camphill Communities his job was to clear the table and sweep the floor after meals, which seemed reasonable as he made the most mess. His passion for clearing up is most apparent when he is in a hurry for the next activity. At such times, if those who are still eating at the table blink, they are likely to find that their plates have been removed and stacked. You have to watch for the signs and hold tight to your plate if you wish to finish your meal!

Golden Handshakes.
Knowing where to start writing this section is as difficult as knowing where to start in dealing with the real

situation. A word of explanation might be in order. Apply a literal, rather than metaphorical interpretation to the expression, then allow your imagination to take over and you are on the right track. We affectionately hijacked this phrase because it so perfectly illustrated the presentation, by Daniel, of the contents of his nappies. I wouldn't wish to put anyone off lunch but this section has to be included as it was a major problem for many years and even now Golden Handshakes are not outside the bounds of possibility. Our earlier attempts at containing (literally) the problem were in the daytime to be super vigilant and try not to let him out of sight. He soon discovered, however, that a quick glance from us into the lounge, wouldn't disclose him in the act behind the chair in the corner of the room. At night we devised a devious method of securing him in his all in one sleep suit. We cunningly put it on him back to front. For a time this was quite effective but once he had broken the code he unzipped himself like a banana and frequently at break of day we would find ourselves scrubbing and disinfecting the bedroom walls after his attempts at re-decorating his room. What a wonderful start to the day that was. One of my most graphic pictures is of the day his bowels reacted to a particular antibiotic. This was obviously quite a challenge for Daniel who, at five years old, still insisted on bringing it to me. The scene that followed had to be seen to be believed. As I ran to investigate the bumping noise coming from the passage there, at the bottom of the stairs was Daniel, lubricated from head to foot in a diluted form of his usual offering, having slid all the way down. As I said earlier, knowing where to start would have been an advantage. Should I check for broken limbs or bumps and bruises, or get the hosepipe out? Fortunately he wasn't hurt and I managed to slither him back up the stairs to the bathroom but for a moment the priority was not very clear. It certainly gave new meaning to the expression 'bowel movement'. On one of his reports from his house parent in Camphill we read "Daniel has thrown his faeces out of the window and given himself a shower, which is a step in the right direction". I'm quite sure that anyone misfortunate enough to be passing the window at that time would feel far from having taken a step in the right direction. It's hard to believe that there could ever be a lesson to be learned from a 'golden handshake' but Matthew has found more than once that he has been able to put his experience to good use. When any of his friends have bemoaned their lot in life he has swiftly been able to put their problems into sharp perspective by telling them that only when they have cleaned their teeth first and then discovered 'poo' on the tap can they claim to have suffered real trauma. There have been so many 'golden handshakes' over the years and it would be so good to be able to say they are a thing of the past but sadly that would be just wishful thinking. It's encouraging to discover, however, that at the age of fifty-four, my reactions are as swift as ever, although I do wish that Daniel wouldn't feel the need to test them in quite that way.

Noah's Ark
I imagine most families with young children end up with an assortment of pets over a period of time and we were no exception. Matthew's passion for animals spanned

the period from age two to eighteen which included a Saturday job in a pet shop so everything from goldfish, mice, hamsters, gerbils, guinea pigs, white rats, stick insects, rabbits, cat, dogs and cockatiel all shared our family home though thankfully not all at once. Daniel took very little interest in any of them except for rare occasions when it would have been much healthier for the pets had he retained his disinterest. The first to succumb was Matthew's pet goldfish who met his fate in Daniel's tightly clenched fist. I had the misfortune to discover the deadly deed when I came downstairs one morning to find an empty fish tank and Daniel sitting on the settee with the contents in his hand, which was offered to me as proof. One snug but very deceased goldfish had to be presented to its' owner who was still sound asleep and blissfully unaware that his little brother had murdered his pet. This wasn't the only time a felony was committed. A new baby guinea pig named Marmaduke only lasted an afternoon. Daniel's usual complete unconcern for animals meant that we didn't really have to worry about their welfare – although we perhaps should have learned from the fish experience – so we were taken off guard when we found Marmaduke's cage door open. Our assumption was that he had been set free by a philanthropic Daniel and we were all set to search the house for the escapee. How naïve we were! On closer examination in the cage we found a little, lifeless form and never quite knew whether he had experienced a similar fate to the fish or simply died of shock at the prospect but his freedom turned out to be from this world rather than from his cage as we had originally thought.

We have had two Border Collie dogs during Daniel's lifetime. Jamie, our first, was part of the family before Daniel arrived so he was well established in the household and had the chance to respond to training in his formative years without the disruptive influence of Daniel in his prime. Bonnie, however, was disadvantaged from the start, coming on the scene when Daniel was ten and already established as 'top dog'. She had to fight for her place and the two of them had a unique relationship consisting of Daniel initiating her mischief by deliberately offering her his cuddly toys, which she would happily rampage with and eventually ravage until the stuffing was all over the floor. He would then revel in her being reprimanded and seemed to gain more pleasure from that than he did from the toys themselves. His positive experiences with our dogs meant that he was quite at ease with other dogs generally and in particular with the Irish Setter and rather large 'other' dog which belonged to our good friend Flo, Daniel's Head Teacher, who lived in the same village as us. She knew Daniel very well and in her wonderful generosity would often offer to have him at her home while we went to church, just to give us a break. Now the state of panic is not something to be generally associated with Flo but came pretty close one Sunday morning when she experienced an uncanny silence in her cottage. She realised to her horror that Daniel and the dogs were nowhere to be seen. The search round the house and garden, then along the lane was in vain and the potential for mischief between them all was overwhelming. Returning from the lane and into the back garden, no doubt with the newspaper headlines flashing through her mind 'head teacher loses boy and dogs' she glanced into her son's car which was temporarily off the road for repairs. There, all seat-belted in and ready to go was Daniel, in the driver's seat of course, Hercules, the Irish Setter in the passenger seat and Mally, the other large dog in the back. Where else would they all be on a Sunday morning and why wouldn't Flo have thought of that. She was a Head Teacher after all!

Who left the door unlocked?
As soon as Daniel grew tall enough to reach door handles a whole new world opened up to him. Each room was an Aladdin's cave as he swept through in search of suitable 'kite' material. We quickly came to the conclusion that we needed to give ourselves a head start and so simple hook and eye locks were fitted to the tops of all the doors. Almost as quickly Daniel, resourceful as ever, was devising means of breaching our attempts at security. The first evidence of this was our frequent discovery of opened bedroom doors and 'Danielised' (a family term which these days would perhaps be 'trashed' but to us needed no further explanation) rooms. It was quite a while, and several accusations of each other leaving the doors unlocked, before we spotted the real culprit in action. We had converted the loft into a playroom for Matthew and when the loft was in use the ladder was left down. Daniel's commitment to get what he wanted enabled him to see the potential in the ladder which was conveniently located to give him access, with just a bit of a stretch, to all the bedroom doors from the third step up. When the ladder wasn't at his disposal he

used a variety of means from knitting needles to the toilet brush to unhinge the locks. Another plot foiled.

Life was and still is full of unexpected surprises when Daniel is around. Picture this scene. There is a knock at the front door and as I open it I am greeted by a slightly embarrassed postman who hands me my 'bra' which he has retrieved from the front lawn after Daniel has hurled it out of the bedroom window. He wasn't the only one who was embarrassed. Then there was the day I went outside to hang the washing on the line and stood quietly contemplating the sight of every piece of the rotary washing line hanging limply from the pole, having been severed by Daniel who is very accomplished with a pair of scissors. Often I would find an assortment of teddies, bound and gagged with sellotape, for reasons best known only to himself. One day my neighbour called and suggested I look out of the bedroom window, from where I could see that her patio resembled a teddy bears' picnic. Every teddy and other soft toy he possessed had been propelled over the fence into Jan's garden. Once again I looked on in bewilderment. While on the subject of teddies it is worth mentioning Daniel's artistic talent that emerged one Christmas when we were visiting my sister, Hazel and her family. We had bought our eldest niece, Caroline, a lampshade in the fashionable care-bears design of the time. After the opening of the Christmas presents Caroline took hers up to her bedroom for safe- keeping – a contradiction in terms when Daniel is around, but one has to try. Silence is very rarely golden when related to Daniel and when everything seemed too quiet it didn't take long to realise that he was missing from the family group. Caroline rushed to her room only to find him just completing his masterpiece of colouring every bear on the lampshade in black felt tip pen. It really was a work of art. She, with us was so astonished at his efforts she couldn't be angry and we promised to buy her a new lampshade. Daniel had never before, or has since, shown any sign of having such ability or desire to colour anything with such precision.

My three nieces, Caroline, Christine and Jennifer, have grown up with Daniel and have survived various traumas from being hoisted from the pram by the bib, hat ribbons or even by their feet, to having their heads patted with weatabix or chocolate pudding covered hands. Their clothes have frequently been relegated to the wardrobe floor as the coat hangers have been commandeered for action. They are grown up now and can all drive so Daniel maintains his vested interest in them as he has at least three options for a ride out in the car. If one of them says no he tries the next until he is successful. The support we have received from my parents and sister and family cannot be measured. It has certainly not been without cost to them, having been subjected to the demands of Daniel as we have, and it will always be appreciated by us.

3 in a bath all lathered up by guess who?

Which one looks most like Father Christmas?

Ground Force

Daniel shared his passion for flowers with his Grandad and me although he had his own unique ideas about garden design that didn't always match ours. I remember with dismay the day I found my newly planted borders laid out horizontally on the footpath in exactly the same order in which I had planted them. It was quite perturbing to see one's beautiful creation scorching to death on the concrete. At least I could replant them and pray for their survival unlike my Dad who had the traumatic experience of finding his prize gladiola beheaded and its' companions in various states of decapitation. All that remained were the tall, gangling green stalks completely bereft of their crowning glory that lay helpless on the grass before them. A similar fate awaited my amaryllis, whose wonderful, stately flower head was doomed to the tabletop and the five feet tall rubber plant that was given a short back and sides or in today's parlance a number 1. Words cannot express the horror of such discoveries especially when one has nurtured the victims with loving care from birth.

Daniel learned a little more respect for the garden during his stay at Camphill and he developed skills as an ace wheel barrower. Forever the opportunist, he wheeled himself off the premises on several occasions. The telltale signs of his abandoned barrow would signal the search that invariably took his co-workers across the adjoining fields in the wild countryside of Kincardineshire. He was sprung on one occasion by the farmer's wife at a local farmhouse whilst attempting to make off with the elastic hair bands of her children. She rang the community to tell them she believed she had one of their residents in her kitchen, if someone would care to collect him! One wonders where he would ever end up if he was not intercepted or caught up with. The extent of his gardening interest these days is watering a few tubs or hanging baskets or helping Linbert to mow the lawn – that is to hold on to the mower, with a wry smile of achievement across his face, while his Dad does the pushing.

'Keep in step Dad and push harder.'

Retail Non-therapy

In Utopia, there would be no shopping with Daniel. However, we all needed to be fed and provided for and it wasn't always possible to do this without his presence. There was no such thing as a mundane shopping trip. It at once comprised of all the things Daniel loved and hated. It had the potential to provide new kites as well as his most un-favourite occupation – queuing. For me it was and still is like being in the vicinity of an unexploded bomb. As a small child, if he wasn't confined to his pushchair or supermarket trolley he would zoom up and down the aisles looking for wooden spoons, balloons or elastic bands while I tried in vain to keep up whilst grabbing the weekly provisions en route. Arrival at the cash desk would herald the awesome discovery that he now had to queue so he would put in place a variety of means in an attempt to thwart the process. The most common tack was to dive to the next cash desk and grab a customer by the collar or handbag, thus causing me to relinquish my place in the queue in order to revive the stunned shopper. He never quite grasped the fact that this manoeuvre caused him to lose ground, as we then had to start the process all over again. I often shopped at the market near our home in North Manchester and one of my most vivid recollections is of a particular day when Daniel was about two years old. He was strapped in his pushchair and parked next to me at the vegetable stall where I was, surprise, surprise, queuing yet again. I had been scanning the array of fruit and vegetables and deciding what to buy when I glanced down at where I had parked Daniel only to find him marching off down the market gripping his pushchair round his waist. Not to be defeated by another queue he had slipped his feet off the foot rest onto the ground then stood up complete with pushchair still strapped to his middle and set off on his mission. Once again my place in the queue was surrendered. I can't remember if we had vegetables that day.

Shoe shopping is a recurring necessity and requires Daniel's presence, if not cooperation. At the time of writing, Daniel is nearly twenty- seven and although quite tall still only looks about fifteen or sixteen. His feet are unusually small which means that after all these years we still find ourselves in the children's shoe department alongside toddlers who in turn find themselves dwarfed by this noisy, relatively huge young man. As his feet are small but very wide, we are not spoiled with a huge choice having usually the option of only one pair to take or leave. We do, however, go through the process of having his feet measured just in case by any fluke of nature they might have grown. This is always a source of amusement to us as we observe the assistant trying her best to keep Daniel's feet flat on the electronic measuring device while he laughs hysterically at her efforts. She probably has to retire to the recovery room after we have left the shop. On one occasion Matthew and Emma came to help me with Daniel, as I didn't feel up to the challenge alone. While the assistant was kneeling at his feet checking the fitting, he was observing from a great height above her when a torrent of his saliva splashed onto her head, travelling along her parting till it became lodged in the start of her ponytail. Emma and I simultaneously dissolved into helpless but stifled laughter leaving Matthew, who fortunately hadn't witnessed the incident, to complete the purchase while attempting to make sense of our behaviour. Thankfully this hasn't been repeated although has the potential to at every fitting, so we are now well prepared with tissues immediately to hand. It is interesting to observe Daniel's complete unwillingness to remove the new shoes from his feet. He thrusts the old pair at the assistant and marches her to the cash desk where he insists they are put in a bag for us to carry home. Nothing will persuade him to carry the bag – his mission is accomplished – if we still have a use for the old shoes that's clearly our problem, not his.

Social Life – What's that?
When Matthew was born in 1974 I was absolutely certain that I wanted to be at home while he was growing up. I wanted to hear his first words and witness his first steps and be the one to influence his development for as long as possible. While it would have helped us financially had I returned to work, childcare was not so accessible or affordable, even on two salaries, and so I followed my instinct to be a full time mother, with no regrets. Daniel arrived two years later, and from then on consumed the largest proportion of my time and energy. Many times, when feeling completely absorbed and overwhelmed with his needs and demands, my commitment to fulltime motherhood waned and I sometimes felt trapped by the lack of choices in my life. Work outside the home was not an option as childcare was not available for someone who needed as much support as Daniel did and even if someone agreed to give it a try they would probably have demanded danger money. I watched my peers being able to move on in their lives as their children became more independent and would often wonder what I might have achieved in terms of a career. However, that was not to be and I learned, albeit sometimes grudgingly, that there could be nothing more important than being instrumental in the

development of another human being – especially one's own son –no matter how hard it may have been at times.

The ordinary things, which would help to maintain balance and sanity in a young mother, such as visiting, having friends round or going out together were such hard work as to be not worth the effort. Visiting or being visited was like a game of pit your wits. Daniel would play to the gallery with his sole motivation being to divert me from anyone who, by means of normal, everyday conversation, was posing a threat to his full time attention. His many aggravating attributes would be on full display as he would empty drawers, cupboards and wardrobes in search of kites, cut up rubber gloves to make elastics and deliberately bring me objects he knew I would have to take away from him. At home eggs would be smashed, cream or toothpaste tubes would be strangled and the contents spread as far as they would reach. Knitting would be unravelled, cereal packets or tins of beans would be carried in and thrust under my nose, visitors handbags or briefcases would be emptied and as a last resort their coats would be brought to them. Had he been able to speak I'm sure he would have said - "this isn't a hint, this is your coat". One visit we had from an educational psychologist has left a lasting impression on me, and quite possibly on him also. He had come to assess Daniel and established from the outset that his policy was to ignore disruptive behaviour. Delinquent parent that I am, the thought crossed my mind "we'll see how long that philosophy holds out". True to form, Daniel upturned the educational psychologist's briefcase and proceeded to snap all the 'unbreakable' educational toys. Finally, his farewell gift was to swot the psychologist's head with a bunch of dead daffodils that I had put in the pedal bin that morning. With yellow pollen scattered all over his black suit I just couldn't resist asking at what point he would stop ignoring such disruptive behaviour.

Daniel is expert at catching you off guard as I was reminded one day when I could hear the all too familiar tune of his little Cassio keyboard yet had a deep sense of something being not quite right in the camp. My intuition hadn't failed me. An investigation into his whereabouts revealed the horror of what he had been up to. There he was, sitting in the middle of Matthew's bed surrounded by every single key from Matthew's much larger keyboard. Anger and disbelief were vying for the predominant place in my emotions and Matthew was understandably just plain hopping mad! That afternoon found me at Dixon's electrical shop with a bald keyboard and a bag full of keys asking wistfully if anything could be done. The assistant casually took the ill-fated instrument and said he would ring to tell me when it was ready. He is to be commended for his professionalism because I'm sure he must have been thinking 'it takes all kinds'! To Matthew and me it presented not just another infuriating inconvenience but yet again the question 'why'?

Nessun Dorma - (or) - Non Shall Sleep.
When Daniel was a baby we could never have imagined how appropriate this title would eventually be. He was very placid and often slept through what should have been a feed time. As the process was such an effort in the early days it would have been tempting to let him

70

wake naturally for his feed but after consulting the Doctor about the situation we both concluded that it was more important for him to get the right nourishment, particularly considering his difficult start in life. As he grew older his sleep pattern became increasingly erratic and in my ignorance I blamed myself for having established this by waking him even though at the time I believed, as did the Doctor, that it was the right thing to do. I have since learned that 'placid' is often a characteristic of early autism and 'erratic sleep' is definitely one of the characteristics of Smith-Magenis Syndrome but I guess my ignorance of this at the time would have had no bearing on the outcome – he still didn't sleep! Even on an elephant's dose of sleeping medication Daniel would only average about six hours sleep a night, which the doctors over the years seemed to feel was quite reasonable. I have to say it didn't feel terribly reasonable when he went to bed at seven in the evening and was up and raring to go at one in the morning. I should perhaps have been grateful as he grew older and his bedtimes became later, giving us till perhaps three or four in the morning, but that gain was often outweighed by the sheer exhaustion of keeping him up and entertained till ten or eleven at night. His idea of occupying himself in the wee small hours ranged from stripping the wallpaper, digging through the plaster to the brickwork of his bedroom wall, emptying his nappy to use as art deco on his wall, tearing clothes, emptying toothpaste tubes and snapping coat hangers to name but a few of the works of his hands. Some things haven't changed much. In his current adult placement he has destroyed all the coat hangers in the house, made kites out of the shelves in the airing cupboard, torn almost all his clothes and bedding and pulled two ceiling roses and light bulb holders, complete with lampshades from the ceiling. There are so many un-answered or perhaps more accurately, un-answerable questions.

Respite Care – One of the greatest innovations of all time
This service was first offered to us in Manchester when it became apparent that we as a family needed to have some time without the pressure of Daniel. It was suggested that Daniel might fit better in a 'foster' family situation rather than in a more institutional environment and while we had reservations as to how he or the potential foster parents might cope we were only too relieved to have some help so decided to give it a try. After a couple of successful teatime visits the family felt able to have Daniel for an overnight stay. We tried to prepare them for all eventualities but we were clearly unsuccessful, as their discovery, in the morning, of a mound of stripped wallpaper in the bedroom signalled his farewell. The second option was short-term care in a purpose built unit at 69 Dickenson Road, which was next door to his school. This proved to be much more appropriate and Daniel thoroughly enjoyed his visits to 'sixty nine' as it was known.

Our move to Bedford meant that we had to start the whole respite process over again. Change was difficult enough for Matthew and myself, but even more so for Daniel who hadn't the faintest idea why it should all be happening anyway. The change wasn't quite so drastic for Linbert, having left Manchester fifteen months earlier to start his new job. However, he was still commuting to London every day and rarely home before eight thirty in the evening, as well as being away frequently overnight on business, so I continued to bear the greatest share of Daniel's care on a day to day basis. As I mentioned earlier, social life was non-existent with Daniel around and I found it very difficult to make new friends so when we were offered respite care in the form of 'Foxgloves', a short term unit similar to 'sixty nine' in Manchester we were very relieved. Daniel loved going to Foxgloves and soon established himself as one who would not be forgotten. This was especially true for the deputy officer in charge who once had the humiliating experience of having him bursting into her room as she had just stepped out of the shower, and then dissolving into hysterical laughter and rolling round the floor. Being a good sport she took it all in her stride and joined his hysterics, but only after she had evicted him from her room. In 1987 we were offered respite care within a family home and naturally after our first experience of this in Manchester we were a little apprehensive on behalf of the family who had offered their services. The day the Gibbs family first came to see us we thought would probably be the last as Daniel was on top form, showing his true colours and full repertoire. They had the added nuisance of Bonnie, our Border Collie puppy of just a few weeks who proceeded to chew the laces of the boys shoes. For some strange reason, which we have yet to discover, Ann, Melvin, David, Peter and Philip decided to give Daniel a try and became lifesavers, taking him for a couple of hours twice a week and giving me some blissful time to myself. They would sometimes take Daniel out on a Saturday afternoon and it was always good to know that his behaviour was equally impressive for them as it was for us. They have lasting memories of a walk in Ampthill Park when he tried to unravel a white scarf from the neck of its' lady owner. Dealing with this delicate operation was one thing but Ann and Mel had the privileged knowledge of where Daniel's hands had previously been having spent the last half hour not very successfully wiping the mangled dog deposit from his fingers on the grass in the absence of a wash basin, soap and towel in the middle of the park. Another Saturday afternoon treat (not for them) was to Daniel's school fete, which was to be opened by the then Mayor of Bedford. The dignitary soon found that he had an appendage to his chain in the form of a small boy who had obviously decided to unfetter him from his rather large and inviting necklace. Once again Ann and Mel were privileged to unhinge him, whilst I'm sure, explaining that he didn't really belong to them. Each time I arrived to collect Daniel from their home I was greeted as the cavalry come to liberate them from near death. As I loaded him into the car they would mop their fevered brows and suggest a six month recovery period. It somehow made me feel so much better about my ability to cope! We have been blessed to have had their support over the years and they remain special to us today. These days they look after our cockatiel who, apart from whistling the opening bars of Mozart's Horn Concerto during the evening news programme, a few feathers and scattered seed, is infinitely less trouble.

Church

Daniel has been taken to our church, The Salvation Army, since he was born. As a baby he was no more difficult to manage that than any other baby in the environment of a church service. If only life had remained that simple. His extreme behaviours were generalised across all sections of the community, including church members who were not exempt from a tie or scarf stranglehold, while others who wore a uniform would find themselves detached from their shoulder epaulettes. It could almost be guaranteed that someone wearing a hat would sit in front of us to deliberately tempt providence. Daniel soon perfected the art of hat removal, leaving the hair beneath standing on end. His love of music has always been well catered for in The Salvation Army and the drums in particular provide not only the rhythm, to which he passionately responds, but also drumsticks which make excellent 'kites', as does the conductor's baton. There is always an underlying motive in his interest, which keeps us on our toes.

Church involvement has provided us with many things that enable us to help Daniel in his development. It provides a network of friends who take an interest in him, giving him the opportunity to form relationships with people, albeit on his own, limited terms and ourselves the chance to encourage socially acceptable behaviours such as shaking hands rather than grabbing clothes – the success of this being open to question, especially by those members who have been on the receiving end of his grip. A greater challenge these days is to educate people to keep hold of their tea and coffee cups at refreshment times. The formal aspect of the service encourages Daniel to sit quietly. His preferred activity, however, is to swing wildly to the music. The expanse of the swing and the velocity of the inevitable dribble from his mouth becoming greater the more excited he gets. Those sitting nearby would be wise to pray for quiet hymns or bring an umbrella.

As Daniel has difficulty with the concept of time, the routine of going to church gives some added structure to his week. When he is told that today is Sunday and he goes to church, he is able to anticipate what the day will bring and this gives him much needed structure and security. Anyone challenging the value of church attendance of a person with the degree of learning disability that Daniel has must also challenge the value of such a person being included in any aspect of the community. An evening in the local pub or a night at the disco can't compete with the variety of experiences offered through a church and as parents we consistently try to reinforce these positive aspects to people who have an input into Daniel's life.

Any organisation be it religious, cultural or recreational, has its values and conditions, the understanding and acceptance of which is essential to membership. This implies that anyone who cannot understand these conditions cannot be a member. While in its' narrow sense this is true, the wider definition of belonging usually applies in most churches. Certainly in our church Daniel has always been accepted as one of the 'family'. However, from the earliest years onwards, this acceptance couldn't protect us as parents from the pain of watching other children and later as young adults taking part in services, becoming members of the various groups within the church – in effect taking on a specific identity, while Daniel remained very much on the edge of everything because of his disability. Special occasions, such as the Sunday School prize giving, were always a source of extreme pain for me as they reinforced the difference between Daniel and other children. These times were particularly poignant when he was given a prize in order to include him in a group with others, with whom in reality, he had not been a part of. The sense of difference continues to be reinforced as young people grow into adulthood and are able to experience the normal rites of passage such as marriage and parenthood. We have at least had the joy of seeing Matthew going through these stages and were so proud to be able to include Daniel, who, while he couldn't be the actual best man at Matt and Emma's wedding (his Dad had that honour) could at least present the rings in the ceremony and did so with admirable decorum – even though he had stripped his buttonhole rose to the stalk and left the petals on my knee. We have since been blessed with a beautiful Granddaughter, Anais who is now two years old. It has been wonderful to see the bond developing between uncle and niece, albeit slightly different from the norm, and a real joy to witness his interest and uncharacteristic gentle approach to her. She clearly had the potential to be seen by him as a real threat to his attention from Matthew particularly, and us generally, and we were not sure which direction things would take. Anais has equally had to make some adjustments in this relationship and while showing a natural curiosity in Daniel's behaviour, seems happy to accept him as he is. She has much to teach people about non-judgemental attitudes. I wish the same could be said of some of the adults I have come across over the years. As the years go by I am continually reminded that my acceptance of Daniel's disability is an ongoing process and was not simply a one-off decision to come to terms with.

What a smart young man. Posing for a photo with Grandad at Matthew and Emma's wedding.

Anais receives a hug from Daniel. Privileged indeed!

Having acknowledged the tangible life experiences that can be available within a church environment I must also acknowledge the spiritual experience that may be possessed by someone who does not have the intellectual capacity to articulate this. Daniel's inability to express or understand concepts means that the traditional 'religious' ideas and expressions are not appropriate to him, but this doesn't mean that he cannot experience his own divine spark or spiritual dimension. My first real challenge in understanding this came as a result of attending Daniel's Sunday service in the Camphill Community in Scotland. It was a very sombre, structured service, although very tranquil, with dim lighting and candles and quite different to what I was used to. I wondered what Daniel felt about it given his propensity for dancing and swinging in the aisles. Over the years I have attended many such services and consistently witnessed the calming effect on many young people who normally exhibit some extreme and bizarre behaviours. It became very clear to me that assumptions cannot be made about a person's spiritual dimension and this realisation challenged my thinking, as to my shame I had majored on the outward experiences that were available to Daniel through the church, ignoring the possibility of anything deeper. The knowledge that Daniel was and is capable of experiencing this deeper dimension to his life, albeit unexpressed in words, gives me a real sense of peace. I have learned much from my involvement with Camphill, whose philosophy is based on the words of Rudolf Steiner, who said "all people, whatever their mental or physical condition, are more than a body, more than a set of emotions, more than words or achievements, they carry an infinite and eternal spiritual being". The application of this means that the needs of the whole person are recognised and supported and importantly, the spiritual being in each person is acknowledged and addressed.

I am very aware that many of the caring people who help to look after Daniel do not profess a particular faith and are not themselves churchgoers, but an awareness of a spiritual dimension to life can be experienced by anyone and even the most severely learning disabled person is capable of experiencing a wholeness of personality if given the right opportunity and guidance. It is our hope as parents that this important area of Daniel's life is not ignored or neglected when we are no longer around to encourage it.

Bereavement
To conclude this chapter I want to share my thoughts on bereavement, an inevitable part of anyone's life. The loss of a loved one is always a difficult time but can bring extra concerns when faced with the prospect of trying to explain to someone who has conceptual difficulties, that a person who may have played a significant role in their life is no longer here. My father was a special person to everyone in our family. He played an important role in each of our lives, including Daniel's and features significantly in many of the anecdotes in this book. When he died in July 2000 I not only had to deal with my own deep, personal sense of loss, but also had to carefully consider how to explain to Daniel that his Granddad had died.

During the time of Dad's illness we took Daniel to visit him in hospital but of course this held no significance for him given that he was a seasoned in-patient and out-patient. We considered it completely unwise to make any connection between hospital and death. Daniel's lack of understanding of the concept of death needed specific action in order to help him form his own concept. After much thought, Linbert and I decided that the best way to do this was to take him to see Dad in the chapel of rest. He joined the rest of the family in this and was able to register that his Grandad was not as he usually was. He also witnessed the emotions of the family and although he was unable to express his feelings he clearly experienced something by his quiet, calm intense observation. The funeral director was very sensitive to our unique situation and suggested it may help for Daniel to see the casket closed and the flowers placed on top. This would give him a picture to recall and hopefully help him to make the connection when he attended the funeral the next morning. If his behaviour in the service was any measure of his understanding then I believe that our decision to take him to see Dad had been the right one. He was extremely calm and touchingly reached out to gently touch the flowers on the coffin, with no intent to pluck one as might easily have been the case. His only apparent relapse was as we left the service when he just couldn't help having a swing to the music. Dad would have appreciated that.

If I have any advice for others who may be preparing to deal with bereavement it is never to assume that a person with learning disabilities does not feel or grieve just because they do not behave in the expected way. Give them opportunities to form their own concept of death and experience the usual stages of grief such as denial, anger or depression even if these emotions are not very obvious. Be alert to changes in behaviour, which may be indicative of unexpressed or unrecognised feelings related to the loss of the loved one and try not to take it too personally if, as in Daniel's case, the person is never referred to again. It may be that there has been a complete acceptance or resignation to the situation or simply that this is how Daniel copes with it, but he has never mentioned Dad or looked for him when we visit Mum. He does however, get great pleasure from looking at photographs, which perhaps keep his memory alive and provide him with some security. We will never know for sure. (But as always we can only do what we feel is best for him).

Chapter 4

OUT AND ABOUT

A walk on the wild side

Daniel enjoys the process of going out, although his cooperation on arrival can never be guaranteed. The journey is clearly more exciting than the destination. One of the activities that can be done without too much organisation is walking and, apart from driving aimlessly around in the car, comes closest to his ideal of travelling rather than arriving. You may already have an image of a leisurely stroll through the park or in the countryside with children running freely and dogs chasing sticks, or perhaps a hike up the hillside or a saunter along the riverbank. For anyone who has ever been out walking with Daniel the reality is likely to be rather less romantic than the image. To have any chance of avoiding the pitfalls one would need the perception or, as I call it, a sixth sense- that Daniel has, plus more than a little speed and wits. I have proved on many occasions in the past and continue to be reminded even now that I do not possess this gift in sufficient measure to outwit him.

Health Warning – Not for the faint hearted or weak stomached

One of Daniel's less socially acceptable behaviours involved his preoccupation with faeces ranging from his own to dogs, donkeys, sheep and cows. Anything, in fact, of a consistency suitable for kneading through his fingers was detected with the eye of a sleuth and scooped with alarming speed and belligerence. One had to be extremely vigilant to keep one step ahead as the ace 'poo' detector operated with the commitment of a person seeking coins with a metal detector and the intuition of a water diviner. In fact he looked remarkably like the latter as he invariably carried sticks in his hands. Having Daniel confined to his pushchair was no protection as he had a dog's eye view of the pavement and closer proximity to the offending article than was safe as he proved on a number of occasions when he leaned over the side of the pushchair and with expert precision scooped the jackpot. A harmless little walk could turn into a nightmare in a few short seconds. A lapse of concentration to admire the view would quickly become a moment of regret at the horror of what he was squelching through his fingers and the realisation that it was going to be presented to me.

On these occasions the rest of the walk was spent looking for toilets, streams, anything that might help to make the journey home tolerable at least. My good friend, Patricia will never forget her first visit to us after we had moved to Bedford. Not having been here very long I was still finding my way round the local beauty spots and hadn't yet established which ones had toilet facilities. We took Daniel to a country park where within five minutes of arriving he had performed his usual party trick with professional sleight of hand. This wasn't really the best time to find out that there were no toilets and after trying desperately to wipe his hands on the grass we found ourselves heading for home with Patricia sitting with Daniel in a wrist lock in the back of my car. There are many times when he had to be marched home in disgrace while I, or anyone else who was unfortunate enough to be with us, tried not to breathe and hoped against hope than no-one would see, or smell us.

Let not one cowpat be unturned

While we are on the subject I think I can say that cow dung came a close second to dog's but was infinitely more acceptable in that Daniel's preference was to play hopscotch in the cowpats which at least kept the business on his shoes rather than in his hands. He just could not, and still can't, resist stomping from one pile to another apparently testing the tops for solidity. I don't think he had a morbid preference for soft centres, but rather he was fascinated by the different consistencies and the challenge of guessing if this one would crunch or collapse. Strangely enough though, he was never impressed with the state of his shoes afterwards and would have been quite happy if I had been prepared to clean them with my handkerchief, which I wasn't. The logic in Daniel's actions is not always easy to recognise, which is probably no different from most of us really. In retrospect it might have been wise to fill a bath before we left the house to go for a walk but fortunately not all excursions necessitated a sheep dip operation afterwards.

Duck – oops, too late

One of our regular places to visit was Bromham Mill on the banks of the River Great Ouse. This is situated just a couple of miles outside of Bedford and is one of a number of lovely walks and picnic areas in the locality. In keeping with his true identity Daniel had no interest in the mill, the scenery or even in having a picnic. He was solely involved in gathering new sticks on the pretext of feeding the ducks. Indeed, frequently, the only motivating factor for him to leave the comfort of the car would be his need for new sticks. If he was content with the old ones, wild horses wouldn't move him. On those occasions when he conceded to get out and feed the ducks one had the distinct feeling that he was doing so to humour the adults. Whole slices of bread would be hurled into the water and Daniel's only obvious pleasure in this was to witness the ensuing battle as all the ducks dived for that one piece of bread as though their lives depended on it. The ducks were used to being fed and would usually anticipate food as soon as humans approached and would trustingly welcome their benefactors as long lost friends and join them on the riverbank. Daniel was usually unimpressed with their performance and went about his hobby of searching for new sticks or redesigning old ones. He has a unique ability to lull one into a sense of false security and it's easy to be caught napping particularly when he seems to be well and truly absorbed in his own world. This is a very dangerous assumption to make. Appearances can be deceptive as my parents experienced. They were nonchalantly standing on the bank, surrounded by devoted ducks. Daniel seemed preoccupied with a new stick, when in a flash, a poor unsuspecting duck found itself lofted from the ground in a vice like neck lock. After a great deal of protest by the duck, Dad managed to release the poor bird to freedom. Strangely enough, next time we visited Bromham Mill there wasn't a duck to be seen. I guess they were all in therapy.

Stampede

We had daily walks across our local fields with Bonnie, our Border Collie dog and when my Mum and Dad came to visit they brought their dog Clyde, who was Bonnie's brother. There were cows in the fields but Daniel paid no obvious attention to them, being, as I said earlier, more interested in their deposits. We always put the dogs on their leads when in close proximity to the cattle. This wasn't so much for the protection of the cows but rather to stop the dogs fleeing for the safety of home, being terrified as they were of the beasts of the field. It was as Dad and I were securing our petrified pets one day that Daniel took advantage of our preoccupation. With turbo charged legs he ran into the herd of peacefully grazing cattle, whacking their rear ends and sending them stampeding down the field in a frenzy. As Dad and I were in charge of a dog each and unable to take any action, we watched in amazement as Mum took responsibility for the situation and staunchly trod between cows and cowpats to retrieve her militant Grandson. I'm not sure what shocked Dad and I most, the stampede or the fact that Mum, who was normally very quiet and unassuming, had taken such control. We should have known that the potential for mischief lay with Daniel rather than the dogs. Yet another peaceful afternoon walk!

Defeat to the seatbelt
After our move to Bedford my parents visited as often as possible and Daniel loved to go out in his Granddad's car. As with our walks, rarely would these adventures be uneventful. Daniel could outwit Houdini any day when it came to slipping his seatbelt. One day, as Granddad was driving along a busy main road, he suddenly found his vision severely impaired by two little hands that were covering each of his eyes. Reeling from shock he speedily removed the obstruction, adjusted his focus and position in the road then proceeded to berate Daniel for undoing his seatbelt, only to realise that in fact the belt was still securely fastened, albeit minus its' passenger. A further defeat or perhaps more appropriately, de-feet, came when Grandma happened to glance in the wing mirror only to see a pair of legs sticking horizontally out of the rear side window. Once again the seatbelt remained intact although its' function was somewhat impaired. We cannot recall how many shoes met their fate on the roadside having been lobbed through the car window, or kites, having outlived their purpose, ended their days alone in a hedgerow.

It is Daniel's phenomenal speed and propensity for unpredictability that makes being out with him so challenging. Even when you think you are aware of all the potential perils there will be a chink in the armour and another attack launched. It is at times like this when you wish you had the apparent sixth sense that he has. People, cars, windscreen wipers (which make excellent kites), walking sticks, bags or clothing are all targets for his attention. We remember well the day my Dad was carrying him back to the car after a shopping trip. He was eyeing the world from a strategic vantage point over Dad's shoulder, when Dad's attention was alerted by a shriek, the kind of sound that was becoming increasingly familiar to us. It is difficult to know who was the most bewildered at the cause of the outburst, Dad or the innocent passer by who had suddenly become bereft of her hat and found it being wafted aloft in front of her as this stranger, in charge of a paediatric delinquent, strode along the pavement.

Frequently I would look back on an activity and wonder why on earth I did that. This is true of a train journey from our home in Manchester to Southport where my parents were living at the time. Daniel was about six years old and I thought it might be quite an adventure for him to travel by train rather than by car, as we would normally do. Not quite brave enough to embark on this alone I enlisted the help of my long-suffering friend Patricia who was foolishly game for some excitement. Would she ever learn? We had Daniel sandwiched between us on the train and for most of the journey he was up and down on the seat constantly checking on the people behind us with his mischievous curiosity. The plan of action became crystal clear after the event. His continual activity of peering over the back of the seat had obviously been for the purpose of disarming his fellow travellers who were by now quite used to the little face which intermittently observed them. We discovered later that one of the people behind us had been reading a newspaper and may well have been working hard not to be too distracted by the constant appearance of 'eyeballs in the sky'. Suddenly, with his usual speed and precision, akin to a magician whipping a table cloth from under its' crockery, Daniel extracted the broadsheet newspaper from the hands of its bewildered owner. It was over the back of our seat in a flash and he sat down with it in exactly the same position he had taken it. The dispossessed owner said nothing as he was probably trying to compute what had just happened, whilst his hands were still positioned as though holding a by now non-existent newspaper. Patricia and I were equally bemused and even more amused as we tried desperately to retrieve the paper in a wholesome state. Daniel of course took complete advantage of the panic and with an evil grin proceeded to rearrange it beyond recognition. How we managed to return it to its rightful owner I don't know but for the rest of the journey all we could do was try and stifle our hysterical laughter as we could hear the gentleman patiently trying to straighten out the crumpled mass. Sometimes laughter, however inappropriate, was the only resort we had.

Whilst in retrospect we can often see the humour in situations this isn't always the case, as a more recent incident confirms. Matthew's fiancé Emma, now our daughter-in-law, came to spend a weekend with us while Matthew was away at Summer Camp in California. She heroically chose to visit while Daniel was at home for the summer holidays so she could get to know him a bit better. A weekend may not seem a long enough time to get to know someone but a weekend spent with Daniel can give someone a very good idea of his potential. You quickly learn to sharpen your wits and reflexes and to expect the unexpected. Emma was in her final year at university studying speech and language therapy and was quite at ease communicating with Daniel. He is always quick to spot those people who are reasonably comfortable with him. Those who are definitely ill at ease will, as his school report says, 'witness his most questionable behaviour'. Fortunately Emma met with his required standards and had a reasonably easy passage. When the time came for her to go home I took her to the railway station and of course Daniel came along for the ride. I took a calculated risk by taking him on to the platform in order to see her off. This was a mistake. Emma's train was the second one due in, which obviously meant that one came in and went out without her getting on it. This clearly threw a spanner in the works for Daniel, although his discomfort with the situation wasn't immediately apparent. I was in the process of explaining to him that Emma would be getting on the next train, when he suddenly launched himself towards a lady who was sitting on her upright suitcase. This was a precarious position at the best of times and this was probably the worst of times as Daniel grabbed her sleeve causing her to wobble uncontrollably. It could only have been providence that kept her from sprawling across the platform and my heart was pounding as I released his grip and apologised profusely for the trauma she had experienced. We moved swiftly up towards the end of the platform, supposedly away from temptation, when he once again lurched towards another lady who was locked in conversation with a friend. He grabbed her sleeve and she swung round in defence and for one horrible moment I thought Daniel would be knocked out flat. Fortunately, she realised in time what the situation was, but things could have been very different.

It is difficult enough dealing with Daniel's bizarre and sometimes frightening behaviour when it involves people we know but when strangers are the recipients it is doubly difficult to cope with. All kinds of emotions come into play. Embarrassment, fear of damage to people or their belongings, fear of repercussions from victims and anxiety about what they themselves might be feeling. I have also to deal with the acute anger and frustration with myself for not having read the signs and anticipated that there could be a potential problem. Then there is the disappointment that having given him the benefit of the doubt, it turns out to be the same old story and nothing has changed. I guess after twenty-seven years as parents we are still puzzled by his actions so it's hardly surprising that others look on in amazement.

Holidays – for whom?
In the early days our philosophy had been to do 'normal' activities with Daniel, which included family holidays. We made our decisions about where to go based on our wishes and economic circumstances rather than what would be best for Daniel. It took a number of years and quite a few holiday experiences to realise that for people on the autistic spectrum, variety is definitely not the spice of life. Our most vivid holiday recollections centre around the time of Daniel's life from age four onwards when his obsession with sticks was becoming more

apparent and intense. From that time his whole focus seems to have been on satisfying his obsession, or hobby, as we prefer to call it. We have been camping, stayed in caravans, cottages and apartments both in the United Kingdom and abroad. It was when the boys were quite young that we tried camping and the memories of those adventures are what make me wonder not only why we thought of doing it at all, but why on earth we did it more than once. I guess all along we have tried to keep a spirit of optimism so we held on to the hope that things might be different next time. Life is a definite learning curve!

Our first camping holiday was in Mablethorpe in Lincolnshire. Once Daniel had familiarised himself with the campsite and located the sandpit it was all down hill. At four o'clock in the morning we would be woken by the sound of the zip on the door flap of the tent and be just in time to see a pair of ankles, the last bit of his little body to be squeezed through the gap as he attempted to embark on his expedition across the pitch black field, complete with his bucket and spade, to the sandpit. Someone had to be on sentry duty every night after that. Our neighbours in a touring caravan took quite an interest in Daniel and invited him in one morning. We tried to explain that this wasn't a good idea but they insisted that he would be fine. As was so often the case with people looking in from the outside, they probably thought that we were being over-protective parents. Daniel needed no encouragement to satisfy his curiosity and took up the invitation with relish. Linbert and I had hardly time to commence countdown when Daniel was evicted having emptied the contents of the cornflake packet all over the caravan floor. It was difficult to curb the urge to say 'I told you so' but we managed, and were not taken up on our offer to help clear up the mess. Perhaps a lesson had been learned by the good hearted neighbours but I suspect not and in a way it would be sad to think that this incident might prejudice their future approaches to people with learning disabilities. Our second and final attempt at camping served to confirm that the whole adventure was not worth it. Daniel needed constant supervision so trying to erect a tent with one eye on him all the time was a nightmare. Then being up before the crack of dawn trying to dry a urine sodden sleeping bag was beyond a joke and definitely not much like a holiday. The tent went up for sale when we returned home.

Our failed camping experiences directed us mainly towards cottage holidays, which are technically supposed to be home from home and as far as Daniel's behaviour is concerned that would seem to be true. A cottage in the country sounds idyllic but there is always an exception to the rule which is usually proved the moment we arrive. Daniel holds no great respect for property, particularly if certain bits of it might be appropriated to furnish his hobby. His skills as an investigative researcher are well honed on arrival at a new holiday destination and anything that will make a good kite is spotted instantly, followed promptly by potential adornments or embellishments for the kite. It is vital to anticipate his thoughts in order to prevent disasters. So far we have been quite unsuccessful, being in musical terms, at least two beats behind the bar most of the time. One of his first ports of call is the bedroom wardrobe where he will transform the coat hangers into an assortment of kites. The familiar crack like a gunshot is always a sharp reminder that we are yet again too late as we run to desperately try and salvage something on which to hang our clothes for the week. One of our many holidays with my parents was to a cottage in The Cotswolds. On arrival I thought I'd get one step ahead of Daniel so while the others unloaded the car, I ran upstairs to remove the coat hangers before they became

Taking Grandma and Grandad for a walk.

mutated. Having successfully completed this mission and feeling quite pleased that on this occasion I had outwitted my son, I went downstairs to announce the good news, only to find my mother carefully untying the knot in the pendulum of the clock, while Daniel stood, arms folded, watching disdainfully as she attempted to reverse his engineering feat. We hadn't been there more than five minutes before the clock was ceremonially removed and put away for safe keeping until we were ready to leave again. Mum sat down, mopped her brow and breathed a sigh of relief – for a while. I managed to foil one plot, but the pendulum clock, which was perilously close to doom, would have been a rather expensive failure.

Our holiday cottage in Westmoreland had a most unfortunate coffee table. When Daniel saw it for the first time he must have thought he was in kite heaven. It was a long, low table with a ledge underneath made of wooden slats. During the course of the week, Daniel systematically removed each slat, which we in turn removed from him. Some made it to the end of the week having been put in a place of safety, but others sadly didn't last the course. We discovered that it isn't as easy for us to put things back together as it is for Daniel to take them apart. He is clearly more gifted in this area than we are.

One of Daniel's favourite adornments for his kites is ladies tights which stretch and wrap beautifully round the top of a stick. These items of clothing have to be guarded with one's life because unless they are supporting a pair of legs they will be sought, found and recycled. At the end of a holiday in Northumberland we were in the car ready to leave and just happened to cast a final glance at the cottage only to see, hanging from the bedroom window, Mum's tights like a flag at half-mast. As we had already locked up and returned the key to the owner, Linbert had to stretch up and pull them from the security of the pebbledash wall. They were well and truly air- conditioned by the time they had been retrieved and returned to Mum who was laughing hysterically with the rest of us. It's difficult to assess the success of her attempt at hiding them from Daniel but at least we all had a good laugh.

From Northumberland to Devon – we are a much-travelled family. I woke up one morning in our apartment in Ilfracombe and found to my horror that Daniel had made cake doilies out of the net curtains. I'm not sure which was worse, the discovery of his creation or the realisation that somehow I was going to have to return them to their original state. After a couple of hours of embroidery I decided which was worse. Those nets would have made pretty impressive embellishments for his kites. It seems a shame to have deprived him of them.

Having survived several wet and windy British holidays we decided to be adventurous and head abroad for some sunshine. Spain was the chosen destination in March 1986 and although Matthew had travelled by air as a baby this was to be the boys' first real experience of flying. Matthew was excited at the whole prospect of flying and a holiday abroad while Daniel was just excited about going anywhere and couldn't have imagined what going up in the sky could possibly be like. I like the hubbub of airports so it added to my pleasure to share in the fun of it all with the boys. Daniel was suitably impressed with the aircraft itself and Linbert, Matthew and myself could not have anticipated how he would react at the point of take-off. He was absolutely astonished and euphoric and when the plane levelled out he signed 'again'. Clearly the experience was too good to be a one-off, he wanted a repeat performance and we would have been quite happy to repeat it too just to see the look on his face again. The holiday itself was enjoyable for all of us and surprisingly uneventful. We hired a car, which enabled us to see the beautiful mountains of Southern Spain, visit Gibraltar as well as some of the lovely Spanish villages. Daniel was characteristically unimpressed with all of that but tolerated it with good humour. The most lasting memory of Spain is the Cassio keyboard that Matthew had treated himself to from the duty free shop at the airport. Daniel was in awe of this mini, mobile piano, which Matthew generously let him borrow from time to time. Once Daniel had located the demonstration tune button we, and the neighbours became subjects for his serenading and by the end of the week had the tune ringing in our ears. Little did Matthew know that his generous gesture would lead to Daniel completely commandeering the cassio not just for the holiday, but for time immemorial. At the time of writing we are still being entertained and although the cassio has been replaced twice since then, sadly the demonstration tune remains the same. Someone must be doing well in royalties!

Having had reasonable success on our first holiday abroad we were confident in arranging another trip. This time it was to Tunisia in North Africa and Matthew's friend Andrew came with us. Africa sounded really exciting and Tunisia itself was a very different experience in terms of the culture and history of the place. We were soon to be reminded that culture and history held no significance for Daniel therefore, in his thinking, they should be of no interest to us. We wanted to see as much of the area as possible so arranged to go on the organised excursions, which would give us the opportunity to do this – or so we thought. In reality we were whisked round the sights in Tunis by a very single minded Daniel who by now had almost perfected the art of the finger in the middle of one's back. This is not a manoeuvre to be resisted and has guaranteed directional success. The wonderful mosaics in the museum became a blur as we were propelled either by this fast developing skill or became victims of the famous wristlock. Had our imagination stretched as far as Daniel's when we visited the ancient ruins of Carthage, we could have reversed the situation, as it was he who dawdled as he diligently searched for ancient sticks to add to his collection.

Searching for ancient sticks in Carthage.

The local teashop was a real source of amusement, as we had to sit on a raised platform with no chairs, cradling our drinks on our laps. This was quite an art, which Daniel managed better than the rest of us, between his chuckles at the whole odd process. Our time on the beach was dominated by observing the decline and fall of the vendors who persistently tried to sell us kaffiyeh (Arab headdresses) and who for some reason thought Daniel would be a soft touch. I don't think they had ever been so duped before and it was amusing to see them frequently following him up the beach demanding payment for the headscarf they had voluntarily put on his head. Quite unperturbed by their distress, he was no doubt humouring them by keeping it on his head for much longer than he retained any sun hat we tried to get him to wear. Probably the most memorable part of the holiday, at least for Andrew and the waiter in the restaurant, was the day Daniel had crème caramel for desert. This in itself was a 'first' as Daniel didn't usually eat puddings so we were astonished at the speed with which he devoured it. We were equally astonished at the speed it came back, right into the middle of the table in almost the exact shape as it had started out. Linbert calmly gathered up the tablecloth by the four corners, lifted it delicately from the table and presented it to the waiter for disposal – as though this sort of thing happened every day. Once we had established that Daniel was well we turned our attention to Andrew who definitely looked a whiter shade of pale and one could quite easily have thought it was he who had been sick. As usual we resorted to our characteristic response and howled with laughter.

As so much of our time had to be spent supervising Daniel, Linbert and I were only too happy for Matthew to take a friend along on holiday, particularly as he got older and more independent. Our next fun-packed holiday, this time with Paul, was to sunny Majorca. We arrived at Luton Airport and joined the long queue to check in our luggage. As I have said before, a queue to Daniel is rather like a red rag to a bull – see it and charge. As the point of standing in a long line evades him he does so under extreme protest. Only when he had surveyed the scene and noted that this wasn't so much a long line of bodies but of suitcases, all bearing luggage labels attached by stretchy bits of elastic, did life take on new meaning. He systematically worked his way up and down the queue of bewildered fellow travellers requisitioning their luggage labels for kite duty. We have yet to discover if everyone had the right bags when they arrived at their destinations but we were quite sure that they would be hoping that we weren't going to be on the same flight. We had booked an apartment in a holiday complex, which included a swimming pool, restaurant and evening entertainment. We were surprised but very grateful that Daniel was content to sit till quite late in the evenings listening to the music and watching people having fun. Our apartment was on the fifth floor so we were naturally very cautious of Daniel on the balcony but as he had no head for heights there was little risk of him climbing. However, that didn't stop him from throwing his underpants over the edge where they landed shamelessly on the one below, fortunately not on anyone's head. I was only too glad that they were his pants and not mine.

The same sentiment might have been expressed by the Majorcan lady sunbather on the beach who suddenly found her bikini top at full stretch in front of her in the grip of a very determined little hand. Fortunately for her a gallant Matthew came to the rescue and removed his little brother with equal determination and even greater embarrassment. Daniel had been very calculating about this performance. He was playing happily in the sand at the edge of the sea so Linbert and I thought we were safe to go in for a swim. We always had him in sight and in what we thought was a reasonable distance to retrieve him if necessary. What a misjudgement. We didn't calculate how long it would take to run with the sea seeming to deliberately hang on to our legs. There was no way we could out streak Daniel across the beach to where the lady was reclining in the sun. He must have registered her presence at some point previously and decided that the strap of her bikini would look good on his kite. Poor Matthew had the misfortune to be closest to the situation so he had the dubious privilege of retrieving his brother and apologising to the stunned sunbather as she readjusted her clothing – such as it was. As Daniel was small and slightly built for his age he was less of a threat than he might otherwise have been and this enabled Matthew to explain and apologise, albeit in haste. However, as with the problem on the railway station platform, the potential for situations turning nasty is a constant concern for us.

Our only long haul flight with Daniel was when he was eleven and we visited Linbert's parents in Jamaica. For various reasons, not the least of which was the high cost of travel for four of us, plus some hesitation as to the wisdom of a journey like this with Daniel, we hadn't ventured there since Daniel had been born. Hence it was to be the first time his grandparents met him and would be an interesting experience particularly for Linbert's dad, who was blind. We who could see found it difficult enough to prepare ourselves when things started to get active on the 'Daniel' front but to be unable to see the advancing assailant was to be at a distinct disadvantage as Granddad Spencer was to discover. We tried our best to help Daniel understand that his Granddad couldn't see but his impaired ability to imagine, or put himself in another's shoes, made it difficult for him to grasp the concept of blindness, particularly as his Granddad's eyes were obviously open. This meant extra caution on our part when Dad was negotiating his way round the house, as Daniel didn't volunteer to take evasive action and make room – he was used to other people doing that for him. The boot was well and truly on the other foot but it didn't quite fit. By the end of the holiday Granddad had become accustomed to being levitated to great heights as Daniel vaulted onto the bottom of his bed. It was fascinating to watch the relationship develop between Granddad and Grandson in spite of the imbalance in handicap and definite advantage that Daniel had.

It was also interesting to note how well Daniel coped with the climate. The heat seemed to affect him very little. It certainly didn't alter his behaviour. He continued to operate with the acceleration of a high speed locomotive, while we chugged in hot, sweaty pursuit in an attempt to keep up with him. As we were staying with family and were not real tourists we hired a car and found the quiet beaches, which made life easier for all of us. Daniel thoroughly enjoyed the warmth of the sea and was very happy to splash around, even being persuaded to enter up to his waist where he played at jumping over the waves. There were rare moments when he lay down at the water's edge and let the waves gently lap around him. It was quite a sight. We had insisted on his wearing a sunhat, which he attempted to dispose of on a number of occasions, finally succeeding during his waterside sunbathing by permitting, or was it encouraging, it to be washed off his head. It was eventually laid to rest somewhere in the Caribbean Sea.

This is the last time we saw the hat.

As this was a holiday specifically to visit family we had the pleasure of being entertained in the homes of a variety of aunts, uncles, cousins and friends. This kind of non-activity can sometimes be quite soporific but not when in the company of Daniel. A surveillance team has to be set up to protect the home and occupants and on one of our visits when I was on 'D' duty, as we called it, I wandered round the large garden watching Daniel in his familiar position of grubbing around in the undergrowth for new sticks. When he approached me with his fist tightly clenched I wondered what treasure he might have found this time and naively held out my hand, only to be presented with a cockroach. What joy! Having made other long haul flights ourselves in recent years and being reminded of the lack of room, especially in the toilets where he needs supervision, we have decided not to venture forth with Daniel in this way again, unless circumstances absolutely demand it.

Daniel's placement in the Camphill Communities in Scotland necessitated his travelling home by train for the school holidays. With children and young people having to travel the length of the land, sleeper compartments were booked and it was usually with great excitement that these journeys were made. On the morning that Daniel was due to arrive home, Linbert and I would be up at five o'clock to drive to Milton Keynes station to meet our wide-eyed son as he bounced along the platform to greet us. He was invariably followed, at a much more sedate pace, by an ashen looking co-worker who had clearly been up all night with him. The co-worker always looked worse than we felt in spite of our unsociably early start to the day. We were so full of admiration for the young people who took such responsibility for Daniel and others like him. They truly deserved the break they were about to have. Daniel switched very quickly from one part of his life to another and immediately started to sign 'car', 'home', 'cup of tea' and 'walk with the dog to see the cows' all in one breath, if it is possible to sign in a breath. This conversation would continue all the way home and we were in no doubt that the long holiday had well and truly begun. The sleeper would have been more appropriately named non-sleeper or 'nessun dorma', an apt sign for Daniel's bedroom door, given that sleep would be in short supply for the duration of the holiday. When it was time for the return journey there was an interesting, but not surprising, reversal of responses. The co-workers looked relaxed and rested while we, and our fellow parents looked drawn and exhausted and visibly heaved a sigh of relief as the train pulled out of the station. I always had mixed feelings as Daniel left, certainly relief, but also inadequacy that I hadn't been as positive as I might have been or coped particularly well when he was being his usual, often annoying, self. Our last image of him at the end of each holiday was his little head hanging out of the train window until he was hauled in. We often wondered what he was thinking. With the gradual reduction in fares, more recent journeys were made by air. These proved equally exciting for the students and at least much shorter in duration for the exhausted co-workers at the end of term. It was always fascinating to watch the reactions of the other passengers at the sight of a group of young people whose behaviour could seem unorthodox, if not very odd to say the least.

Having returned to a local residential fifty-two week placement, Daniel no longer has the long school holidays so we are able to organise his home visits in shorter, more regular chunks which lightens the load a little. We do still take him on holiday with us and although he is an adult, the challenges persist, perhaps even more so. I constantly have to remind myself that Daniel's disability isn't going to disappear for a week just because I need a break. Indeed his behaviour is likely to be exacerbated by a change of environment. In retrospect, we should have perhaps taken more holidays without him, but with time at a premium and the belief that he needed a holiday just as much as we did, we planned our breaks when he was home for the school holidays. Our first holiday without either of the boys was when Daniel was twenty and it was strange to experience what a holiday could really feel like. We hope to have a few more experiences like that.

We have always tried to maintain a social life, although often against great odds, and Daniel has acquired a variety of recreational interests such as swimming, eating out, live music concerts and ten-pin bowling – although with bowling he thinks the aim is to get the ball in the gully, which he does quite successfully. Swimming, particularly in his younger days, held its' own hazards, although not for him. Swimmers were likely to experience some resistance, and possibly embarrassment in the water, as their swimsuits were grabbed midstream. Another major consideration was the subject of his chronic catarrh, which was aggravated by the chlorine in the water. It doesn't take a vivid imagination to visualise the results of being without tissues in the swimming pool. The upside of this scenario was that we gained more space in the pool. Oddly enough, the acquisition of space seemed to be the rule wherever we were. Parks or beaches, however crowded to start with, usually became much less so in our immediate environment as people gradually edged away. There is some compensation after all.

Don't let go Mum.

Restaurants and teashops have always been Daniel's favourite places to go and it would be good to be able to say that these visits were usually without incident, but not quite correct. Customers are a captive audience with no means of escape and might find themselves subject to an unexpected cabaret act. It could simply be a volcanic explosion of crispy seaweed, which literally goes up like Vesuvius and descends in a haze of green ash all over the tablecloth, or it may be a more elaborate performance as witnessed by the patrons of The Ritz in London. A business colleague of Linbert was visiting from Australia and he and his wife insisted on meeting the family and treating us to dinner in this rather posh hotel. To say that Daniel rose to the occasion would be to state the obvious as that was exactly what he did. We were seated at a long, bench style, plush velvet sofa when he stood up and began to march up and down it, squashing butter pats in his hands and laughing hysterically. Whether he found the environment conducive to theatrical entertainment or just felt that it needed livening up a touch we will never know, but we were completely at a loss to know how to respond. I can remember thinking that this would be the last time we would eat at the Ritz, not that Daniel's outburst would have made the slightest difference to that fact of course. It was, however, an unforgettable experience for us all, especially the Australians.

After this we became a little more selective in our choice of places to eat out. Anywhere, especially garden centres, where there is a teashop will be added to the list of 'possibles' and the more there are the longer each one has to recover between our visits, as we generously rotate between them all. I have been known to do four garden centres in one day without actually seeing anything related to a garden at all, being subject as I am to the finger in my back directing me straight to the teashop. Daniel will refuse point blank to sit down at a table with anyone until the drinks are in place and will insist on queuing, or rather queue jumping in order to supervise the process. I always visualise the whole line of people going down like a row of dominoes. We have come close a few times but fortunately never quite achieved it. He doesn't always choose to eat, but when he does he nearly always opts for a jumbo sausage roll.

I'll leave it to your imagination to picture the scene after we leave the table. Pastry, especially jumbo size, has a voluminous fall-out. We rarely manage to escape the cold drinks cabinet, which is spotted as soon as he enters the shop. He will extract a bottle, which holds more than a can, and place it with the tea on the tray. We have learned not to try and bargain with him over this, as we would never win without a fight and by now we know how to choose our battles. It is never going to be tea or coke but always both and when we are really unlucky he will choose cappuccino coffee in place of tea. The result of this is half a pint of coke, diluted with saliva, plus an inch of cappuccino coffee froth round his face and down his jumper. Sadly we never have a camera with us to capture this image. It isn't something one normally takes to a teashop.

Daniel's real love is music and there's nothing he likes better than to listen to and watch a live music performance. He has been brought up in a musical environment with Linbert, Matthew and myself all playing instruments from piano, guitar and percussion to a variety of brass instruments. Our involvement at the Salvation Army has meant that Daniel has experienced instrumental and vocal music of all types on a regular basis since he was born. One of his favourite musical occasions is the 'Proms in the Park' concert in Bedford Park. The whole idea of sitting in the open air with a flask of tea and an orchestra to entertain him is beyond his wildest dreams, although he gets a bit impatient at having to wait till the end to hear his favourites like Pomp and Circumstance March and Rule Britannia. It was at our first open air concert that we observed that he became very disorientated during the laser display at the end and actually volunteered to sit down rather than stand and swing to the music. We bought him the video of the BBC's Last night of the proms, which he has played and rewound so many times that it has had to be replaced. I cringe at the mere mention of Balshazzar's Feast. He must know every note of it.

The Maestro.

While he was living in the Camphill Community he spent many happy evenings listening to performances of classical and folk music, given by the many talented young co-workers. He developed a liking for Irish folk tunes and had specific favourites, which he identified quite readily. He was also taken to a performance of Handel's Messiah, which apparently enthralled him, and to the opera which held slightly less appeal but which he enjoyed, nevertheless. He had a wonderfully rich cultural life in Camphill which is unlikely to be matched anywhere else. It has always been a source of frustration to us that the policy of care in the community often means that 'access' only stretches as far as the local pub, disco or shops. The kind of cultural activities in which Daniel has been able to take part in the past seem to be alien. While we realise that participation in such activities costs money, it is also dependent upon the interests and availability of care workers. Sadly, the fewer opportunities Daniel has to access these less typical activities the less he will be able to be 'managed', having become un-used to sitting quietly. Not ever sitting quietly could then become a way of behaving and he and others like him will be perceived as unable to cope with what might be seen as more formal events or environments. When Daniel is at home with us we try to ensure that he continues to have as varied a cultural life as possible, but wish that this could be guaranteed for him when we are no longer here to facilitate it.

Chapter 5

NOT ANOTHER HOSPITAL APPOINTMENT

The Waiting Room

"Take a seat please". These were the immortal words that lit the touch paper and sent Daniel rocketing round a waiting room like a Whirling Dervish. If his bottom touched a chair it was only for long enough to survey the scene and decide on the most suitable tactics to achieve his goal, which was either to see the doctor or get out. This he accomplished by a variety of not so subtle means. Scarves, ties, hats, babies, equipment, wheelchairs (preferably occupied), patients records, fish tanks all held a fatal fascination and the potential to serve a very useful function.

It is the latter of this list that stirs the earliest memory of a long line of waiting room horrors. It was the first of many visits to our General Practitioner in North Manchester. The doctor was a quiet, unassuming gentleman who had been caring for the people of that community for many years. The waiting room was quite small and narrow, sparsely furnished apart from a lovely tropical fish tank, the doctor's pride and joy. The fish tank provided a focal point and therapy for the patients who became temporarily distracted from their ailments. At least that was the case prior to our arrival, after which it probably had the opposite effect. Daniel surprisingly took a keen interest in the fish for which I was very grateful, feeling that for once he might actually wait patiently for a while. My optimism was short lived as in a flash he had disconnected the tube from the pump to the tank. For reasons beyond my scientific knowledge, the water, followed closely by miniature tropical fish, was sucked up the tube and gushed out on to the waiting room floor. In no time it resembled a paddling pool. Feet were lifted into the air, with no decorum, the receptionist, who always had such control at her desk, was hysterical while I tried to stem the flow from the tube with my finger whilst keeping hold of Daniel at the same time. Meanwhile, the doctor calmly appeared from his consulting room to see what the commotion was. He sorted the fish tank, calmed the receptionist and set her about mopping the floor, reassured his other patients and took Daniel and I into the consulting room. As we left the surgery a little while later I heard the doctor say to the receptionist "next time Mrs Spencer is here with Daniel, send her straight in". I think Daniel achieved his purpose very effectively that morning. I have to say though, that this was definitely an occasion when the funny side is only seen in retrospect. At the time, my emotions were like a Molotov cocktail. I was panic stricken at the prospect of those tiny fish ending their days on the waiting room floor, red with embarrassment at the sight of the patients with their feet in the air, all sense of dignity lost and bewildered by the hysteria of the previously cool, calm receptionist. I could happily have throttled Daniel. Is that what might be called stress these days, I wonder?

Having gone to such extreme measures to ensure a quick passage in and out of the doctor's surgery, it was apparent all too quickly to Daniel that equally effective tactics would need to be employed to ensure similar success at all subsequent surgeries or hospital waiting rooms. In pre-computerised times, one such measure was the deftly executed removal of the elastic band that secured the order of the patients record cards. In a split second the cards would be scattered in all directions and the previously organised receptionist would find herself in a complete state of disorganisation as she frantically tried to remember, as discretely as possible, the order of arrival of the patients, in order to avoid having a mutiny on her hands. If this ploy didn't get immediate results for Daniel a further option might be to focus on the patients themselves. A quick scan round the room would identify the most vulnerable – those with scarves, ties, walking sticks or better still, those in a wheelchair. A hand clamp round a necktie or scarf could work wonders, although clearly not for the victim. It brought immediate attention from Linbert or myself as we had to delicately but firmly prize open very determined fingers to release the innocent prisoner before he or she turned blue.

An occupied wheelchair held a singularly fatal attraction. The combination of a captive audience and the power to manipulate this super-pushchair was irresistible. At school, Daniel was encouraged to help the children who were in wheelchairs and was often allowed to share the pushing with a teacher. To see someone unattended was too good to be true, an opportunity not to be missed. After all he was only helping! It was not just wheelchairs that provided a source of excitement. I remember one particular visit to Manchester Royal Infirmary when my Dad accompanied me to help with Daniel. It was one of several appointments we had there for Daniel to have grommets inserted into his ears to help clear fluid from the middle ear. This was a recurrent problem and yet another thing for him to cope with. The waiting procedure took place in the play area of the ward, which was full of nervous, vulnerable children who were also awaiting admission. As if that wasn't enough, they found themselves in the company of Daniel who didn't do much to alleviate their anxiety. Their pre-admission play therapy was seriously at risk. At best, toys, jigsaws, drawings, in fact all their creations were targets for destruction. Dolls were dismembered without anaesthetic and action men swiftly became non-action men having undergone amputation. Those children who had returned to the ward from theatre were even more attractive to Daniel and with drips still attached were a great source of interest. It was from this environment that Daniel, still waiting to be seen, was extracted by Dad and taken for a walk along the corridor. Here, something even better than a wheelchair caught his eye. A bed, ready and waiting to take the next patient to theatre, was grabbed with great gusto and propelled with equal speed and determination towards the double swing doors marked 'theatre, no unauthorised entry'. With Dad in hot pursuit and fortunately in good athletic form, the wayward wheely-bed was halted halfway through the doors and retrieved, complete with Daniel. The bed was finally surrendered and with a twinkle in his eye, Daniel took sanctuary in the ladies toilet grinning from ear to ear as he watched his Granddad's expression of relief change to one of disbelief. Dad was just ready to capitulate and come to get me when Daniel recognised the danger signs and gave himself up quietly, although still grinning, and was marched back to the waiting area. I should add at this stage that the wheely-bed had not been occupied at the time of its' abduction, although that fact would not have altered Daniel's intention. It might, however, have made a significant difference to a patient's state of health. When the great moment came and we finally got in to see the doctor, it was just a matter of seconds before the instrument tray was upturned and the contents scattered across the room. Most of the children on the ward were kept in overnight following this particular operation but it didn't take long for the doctor to suggest that once Daniel had recovered from the anaesthetic it would be better if he went home. It's amazing how quickly some decisions can be made.

    With Daniel's unhealthy hobby of turning faeces of any origin into 'golden handshakes' it isn't surprising that he contracted infectious hepatitis and ended up in the isolation hospital. That morning in September 1981 is indelibly printed on my memory. We had moved from North to South Manchester in July at the end of the summer term and this was to be Matthew's first day at his new Junior School at the start of the autumn term. Daniel had been unwell over the weekend, with sickness and loss of appetite but the doctor thought it was just a tummy upset, which would clear in a day or two. I decided to keep him home from school that day but I still had to take Matthew to his new school so I put Daniel in his pushchair and off we went. By the time we arrived at the school gates his eyes were a lovely shade of daffodil yellow and it was obvious that this was no ordinary tummy upset. I couldn't risk taking him into the school in his condition so consequently had to deposit Matthew at the gate and leave him to find his own way in and introduce himself. I remembered the many times I had started a new school and the sick, lonely feeling deep in my stomach at the prospect of having to make new friends and get used to a new environment. I knew that Matthew was feeling apprehensive and I wanted so much to be able to just walk into the school with him, but I couldn't and just prayed that he would be given the courage he would need to get through that first day.

I returned home in great haste to call the doctor who came immediately and sent for an ambulance to take Daniel to the isolation hospital. I had to make swift arrangements for my neighbour, who I hardly knew yet, to collect Matthew from school as Linbert was away on business and I was unlikely to get home from hospital in time. I had yet again to cope with my feelings of guilt at not being there for Matthew because I had to be somewhere else for Daniel. This was proving to be the pattern of things in the family, that Daniel, through no fault of his own, would monopolise our time and energy. He was gifted in hijacking Linbert or myself by creating a situation that required our immediate attention. In fact he didn't even have to create a specific situation, he just had to be there and our attention was diverted. This was how life was and Matthew accepted it with great maturity and remarkable lack of resentment. To return to the story, I travelled with Daniel to the isolation hospital, which was actually in North Manchester not far from where we used to live. We went through the usual admissions trauma and were eventually admitted to an isolation room where Daniel would have to remain until the all clear from infectious hepatitis was given. Apart from his yellow eyes he showed no sign of illness or lethargy, in fact quite the opposite, and as no treatment could be given he was rather perplexed at his incarceration. The very least he expected was that someone would look down his ears, listen to his chest, or give him medicine or an injection – but nothing! There was still, however, the not so insignificant matter of his loose bowels which I was allotted the maternal privilege of dealing with under the guise of 'I think he'd be happier if his Mum did this'. What they really meant was that they would be happier if his Mum did this. I travelled to the hospital every day to be with Daniel and help with his general care. It didn't take longer than the first morning to realise that some reorganisation of the furniture was needed, starting with the cot-bed which he expertly abseiled down, having practiced this skill when he was first in Booth Hall Hospital at the age of three. The safest place for him to sleep was on the floor so I wedged the mattress into the corner of the room. The next priority was to limit his opportunities to escape, so I placed my chair strategically in front of the door as some measure of deterrent. The highlight of his day was mealtimes and he ate as though he would never see another meal again. O course what went in also came out so that kept us both occupied. The week seemed like a month. Added to the strain of trying to entertain Daniel in such a confined space was the physical tiredness of travelling backwards and forwards everyday and the guilt that I hadn't been available for Matthew in his first week at school. Perhaps these things combined to lower my resistance but two weeks later I woke up one morning feeling very unwell and thought that I had 'flu'. Linbert had gone away on business that morning and by lunchtime I had to ring him to come home. I could hardly walk let alone look after Daniel when he came home from school. The doctor was called and took a blood sample, which went for immediate testing. The result confirmed his suspicion that I had infectious hepatitis, which in an adult is a much more debilitating and prolonged disease compared to the childhood version – as I was to find out. The normal procedure would have been admittance to an isolation ward in the hospital but because of the situation with Daniel I was given special dispensation to stay at home, albeit out of contact with anyone other than immediate family who had already been exposed to the disease. With the help of my parents, who had been offered vaccination against hepatitis, and a couple of close friends we coped for the eight weeks that I was ill. Incidentally, Linbert, Matthew and myself, who were in closest proximity to Daniel, were not offered vaccination. Perhaps it was considered too late, but I have often wondered. During the time that Daniel was ill, the most natural response from me was to care for him, without any thought of the consequences. When my family were doing the same for me I became acutely aware of how much time and energy they gave to me notwithstanding the risks to their own health. It was a very high price to pay but I guess that is what life and love are all about. I learned yet another important lesson – caring costs.

We were very grateful over the years for the excellent support we received regarding Daniel's development and well being but this inevitably meant an endless round of appointments ranging from the general monitoring of his progress to the management of his specific health problems. One of the more frequent appointments we had was to the Department of Audiology at Manchester University. Although we didn't think Daniel was deaf, there were times when his responses seemed slow and we could never be sure if he heard us and simply chose not to respond because he was absorbed in something he was doing, or if the level of his hearing was low. As he still had no speech and there was a marked lack of developmental progress, we felt that every avenue had to be pursued in order to eliminate any possible causes and this was one area about which we could make no assumptions and so I took Daniel for the first of many memorable appointments. The room in the clinic was uncluttered, apart from two tables, to ensure that there were no distractions. At one table was seated the audiologist, while the other supported the audiometer, the instrument which measures sensitivity to sounds. The general idea was that one audiologist sat opposite Daniel at the table and attempted to attract his interest in a variety of small toys. While this was taking place, another audiologist, standing behind him, used certain pieces of equipment designed to produce sounds of various pitch and intensity with the intention of measuring the level of his response. This might seem like a simple enough procedure but Daniel was no-one's fool. He had no interest whatsoever in the toys on the table and may just as well have turned his chair round as he spent most of his time in reverse waiting for the silly sounds from behind. In effect, he had the whole thing sussed in one session. I explained that now Daniel knew what to expect that he would never cooperate fully in this situation and that it was unlikely to produce a satisfactory result. My comments clearly fell on deaf ears, if you'll pardon the pun, as a number of follow-up appointments were made at which Daniel made a mockery out of everyone until eventually the significant observation was made that this process was unsuccessful in establishing an accurate measurement of his hearing. I managed to curb the desire to say 'if you had listened to what I said in the beginning we could have saved a lot of time and energy'. I realise that professionals have to be seen to do the best they can but perhaps 'the best' might actually be to listen to an expert, maybe not in their field of expertise, but expert in the one they are trying to help. I wouldn't be so arrogant as to comment on those matters I know nothing about, but I do have considerable experience of Daniel's 'little ways', the knowledge of which can make all the difference to how a situation may be best approached. It seems unwise not to tap into such an obvious resource, but perhaps it's only obvious to me.

There was apparently a more accurate way of obtaining the desired information which was clearly only used as a last resort as it involved performing the test under general anaesthetic. It meant a day in hospital, of course, but we felt that if it resulted in an answer to our question about Daniel's hearing, then it would be worth the stress. The test established that he had a mild to moderate hearing loss and the suggestion was made to try him with a hearing aid. My imagination was filled with a kaleidoscope of images, which proved to be not too far from reality, as time would soon tell. Almost everyday Daniel returned from school with a note from the teacher apologising that he had yet again chewed the ends of the hearing aid tube flat beyond recognition. It was fairly apparent that his learning disability was not caused by or affected by his hearing loss, so after numerous requests for new hearing aids, the decision to abandon them was taken. We came to the conclusion that it was easier and less costly to the National Health Service to just raise our voices.

Coping with life generally can be quite stressful at times and moving house ranks high in the stress factor statistics. Our move from Manchester to Bedford put me fairly high in the stress factor rankings, not just from the business of selling and buying a house and adjusting to all the accompanying changes, but also from the responsibility of trying to help our boys to settle in a completely new environment. The prospect of rebuilding support networks and making new friends was daunting. If the changes were difficult for me who had some measure of control over what was happening, they were immeasurably more difficult for the boys. At least Matthew could understand why the move was necessary even though he hadn't wanted to make it any more than I had, but Daniel had no means of making sense of all these strange new things in his life. His house, school, district, people, doctors, hospitals, church, respite care and even his walks all changed which compounded the everyday stress caused by the frustrations associated with his disability. I have always believed that body, mind and spirit cannot be separated, that each affects the other and that dis-ease of the mind or spirit can cause dis-ease of the body. I'm sure that the stress that Daniel lived with every day contributed to his frequent bouts of poor health. A limited ability to communicate and form meaningful relationships can severely restrict a person's quality of life and often their health suffers as a consequence. In view of this, one of our priorities was to ensure that the previous medical care was continued and soon the transfer to parallel clinics began.

Most of the new appointments took place at the local Child Guidance Centre (CDC), which was situated quite close to home and school, making life a little easier. The reception staff soon got to know Daniel and to accept that his arrival would signal a tornado as he swept through the waiting area. An important feature of the clinic was the proximity of the car park where, on bad days or if the clinic was running late, we could retreat to the car where we would wait for the signal to return. In the early days the appointments alternated between the Ear, Nose and Throat and General Medical specialists who at different times both referred Daniel to see consultants at Bedford Hospital. Our first such appointment was to see the ENT Consultant about Daniel's allergic rhinitis and chronic catarrh, the latter being as big a social problem as medical. He discovered quite early on in life that the contents of his nose, if ejected with a gale force blow without a handkerchief, could be used as a lethal weapon. This action caused an immediate evacuation response from his proximity that would shame the S.A.S. while Linbert or I produced a handkerchief, as if by magic, to rescue the afflicted. The consultant, victim on this occasion, promptly prescribed a nasal spray, before discharging us almost as rapidly as Daniel had his nose. We never did find out what he was allergic to – probably hospitals. It was within our first year in Bedford that Daniel had his first fit. An appointment with the neurologist was made and following an E.E.G. (that meant another head full of clothes pegs) a diagnosis of epilepsy was given. Daniel has been on medication for this condition ever since and fortunately the fits are well controlled. A further referral to the hospital came following the diagnosis of a hiatus hernia. The school doctor had detected sounds of reflux from his stomach to his oesophagus, during a routine health check at school. At this point in time Daniel had shown no obvious signs of discomfort although he had always chosen to eat rather bland foods, refusing anything acid or spicy. He clearly had an awareness of his own body's needs that at the time we hadn't. As time went by he developed more and more obvious symptoms of a hernia. There were increasing occasions when he was vomiting and blood tests showed a gradual decline in his haemoglobin count. The decision was made to perform a gastroscopy and an appointment was soon forthcoming for admission as a day patient. I had by now learned to warn hospitals in advance, of the impending chaos if we had to wait any length of time. There was certainly no way I would be able to keep Daniel in a bed, hospital or not, if his eyes were open. The dreaded day arrived and I took Daniel up to the ward for admission. My heart sank as I looked round and saw the other patients, some waiting anxiously, some recovering but all extremely vulnerable and the last thing they would want would be a hyperactive young man rampaging round their beds. The staff saw the warning signs and fortunately we didn't have to wait too long before Daniel was sedated and ready to go for the examination. I was allowed to go with him and watched the procedure with great interest as well as concern and some trauma as I could see the damage to his oesophagus caused by the acid reflux. I was feeling somewhat washed out by the time we went back to the ward and was assured by the doctor that Daniel would sleep for a while now and I would have an opportunity to regain my strength. I had no sooner sat down on the chair next to his bed, before he jumped up, slid off the bed and streaked up the ward, his white backless hospital gown wafting in the breeze. I'd like to say that I followed him in hot pursuit, but that was only in my mind. My legs were not cooperating with my desire to head him off before he reached the day room. I was in need of a resuscitation unit by the time I retrieved him and in fact it was me who looked as though I had recently had an anaesthetic. Once again the staff decided that we could go home, but ironically the criteria this time was my fitness rather than his. The recommendation following this appointment was to treat the condition with medication at this stage rather than put Daniel through the trauma of surgery at such a young age – he was only eleven. In fact this means of treatment continued for nearly four years.

After Daniel's move to the Camphill School in Scotland his health continued to deteriorate and it was apparent that the medication was insufficient to control the problem of reflux. His blood count was often very low, suggesting that there was now quite considerable bleeding from the ulceration in his oesophagus and he had to be given iron to maintain a reasonable level. His health was monitored by the doctor in Scotland, as well as by the clinic doctor when he was home on holiday. It was while he was home in the summer of 1990 that blood tests confirmed chronic blood loss and so a further gastroscopy was arranged. Once bitten, twice shy, as they say and not feeling inclined to repeat the previous performance I thought it would be wise to have some help this time. As Linbert would have needed to take a full day off work we decided that we should try and conserve his time for when we really needed it should the outcome of the appointment be surgery. All I needed was an extra pair of hands and eyes for an hour or two and was extremely grateful when Daniel's former teacher from the local school was able to spare some time to support me. It was important to have help from someone who knew Daniel well and would be able to take control if I felt unwell again. Once again I went in to watch the procedure and was horrified to see the state of his oesophagus. He must have been in extreme pain and discomfort and had never been able to express it except to refuse food or be sick. I felt congested with feelings of inadequacy and guilt, wondering how much he had suffered without my being aware of it and whether I had been too hard on him when his behaviour had been less than congenial. The doctor had no hesitation in recommending that Daniel be admitted to Great Ormond Street Hospital for surgery. I knew this was the only option, but the thought of how he and we would cope with major surgery and its' aftermath in terms of keeping Daniel confined, filled me with despair.

The appointment for Great Ormond Street Hospital came for January 1991 in order that it could take place during his winter holiday from school in Scotland. Linbert and I took him in the train so the day started with a mixture of excitement and bewilderment for Daniel. He clearly liked the idea of a train journey but wasn't so sure about the hospital bit and why he had to go on a train to get to it. It was reminiscent of the good news and the bad news again. It was yet another occasion when we were at a loss to know how to prepare him for what was to come. After registering our arrival at the hospital Daniel was given his first blood test, which was necessary before his name could be placed on the theatre list for the following day. When the results came back later that afternoon we were told that he would need a blood transfusion, possibly two, as his blood count was too low to risk surgery. As I tried to visualise Daniel lying still on a bed for the duration of a blood transfusion, the memory of my experience in the gastroscopy unit came flooding back. The image turned into reality that evening when the process began. I suggested that his sleeping medication was given to him before the drip was set up to give us a fighting chance of keeping him in bed. I was to stay at the hospital for the duration of Daniel's stay and on this night was given a bed in his room. From eight o'clock that evening till one o'clock in the morning he fought to remove the drip. He fought sleep and he fought anyone including myself who attempted to hold his hands to prevent him pulling the needle out. I was exhausted by the time he finally succumbed to sleep, allowing the transfusion to take its course during what was left of the night. I had fitful sleep, keeping one eye and ear open all night to make sure everything, including Daniel, was still intact. Morning came all too quickly and Daniel was up with the larks and raring to go. I was still in a comatosed state and not in the least bit ready to go anywhere. A further blood test had to be carried out to find the new haemoglobin count and before the result was to hand, another day had gone by.

The following morning the doctor arrived to say that another transfusion was necessary and would be done immediately. This meant coping with Daniel during the daytime when there was no chance of him going to sleep. As I could barely hold myself up I wasn't too optimistic about being able to hold him down. With an occasional break, when a nurse took over for a while, I managed to see this transfusion through and after a further blood test we were given the O.K. for surgery. Just as I was beginning to sigh with relief I was told that unfortunately the surgeon wouldn't be operating for another two days therefore we would have to return home and come back again in two days time. My mind went numb and then raced as I tried to visualise explaining all this to Daniel who would now think it was all over, when actually the worst was still to come. If only the hospital staff realised the implications of what they had said it might have made it a little easier to cope, but I felt that it was just seen as a regrettable but unavoidable inconvenience. Even the dedication and kindness of the staff couldn't compensate for the frustration of having to fit into their system. We had no option but to deal with the anti-climax as best we could and two days later we were back in Great Ormond Street Hospital awaiting Daniel's admission to theatre. The operation wasn't without complications as Daniel apparently had a chest infection, which hadn't been diagnosed before he went into theatre. Daniel had grown up coping with all sorts of ailments that we had not always been aware of, possibly because he had a high pain threshold, and this had been a fairly crucial situation for him to have masked. This time I didn't feel guilty that I had missed something important because the medical team had also missed it, having performed all the usual pre-admission examinations, including listening to his chest. After three hours Daniel was returned to his room where Linbert and I had been anxiously waiting. It is impossible to describe the feelings of relief and gratitude that we had at that moment but we soon registered the fact that he had emerged with two drips attached – double trouble! He woke from the anaesthetic like he wakes from his normal sleep, in record time. Once he had noticed the two foreign bodies in the form of drips, his mission to remove them began in earnest. These things didn't belong in his body and they had to go. He was as focussed on their removal as we had to be on their anchorage. It was exhausting work trying to keep two arms intact and with the best will in the world we had to have breaks from the sheer intensity of it. Busy nursing staff helped from time to time but never fully appreciated what I meant when I said 'you can't let go of his arms,' because every time I came back from a break, the drips were out, there was blood all over the bed and we were then left having to wait for the availability of a doctor to put the needles back in. Daniels's actions to speed up his departure from hospital had the reverse effect, slowing down the process considerably – but how could he be expected to understand that. It was similar to our shopping experiences when his behaviour caused me to lose my place in a queue and we had to start all over again. Making connections is not Daniel's strong point but then I don't necessarily think it is something that people in general are particularly good at.

As I write this chapter in March 2003 I have a sense of déjà vu as our country is on the brink of a Gulf war. The night following Daniel's operation, while Linbert was on 'night duty' and was watching the television in the ward, the first Gulf war was started. We had expended so much emotional and physical energy on Daniel that it was difficult to take in anything extra, especially something of the severity of a war. The whole situation seemed unreal. However, in spite of the political turmoil, life had to go on and our immediate concern was for Daniel's recovery. His stay in hospital seemed like a lifetime but in fact the whole process, including the two days at home, was only two weeks in total. His recovery was excellent and he was a like new person. We were so grateful for all that had been done for Daniel and as we anticipated his return to Camphill, we had the added confidence that Katrin, his wonderful co-worker, who also happened to be a qualified doctor, would be looking after him and keeping a close eye on his progress. Daniel's health continued to improve and so far there have been no major hospital experiences since that time.

Throughout all the above experiences there have been many times when we have wanted to know the 'why', 'what' and 'when' of our situation. Whilst we may have been able to ask the questions we have still been subject to the timing and control of those in charge of the information and process. We who are considered 'normal' often find it necessary to challenge the system but perhaps our socialisation enables us to cope with the uncertainty and to some extent exercise some patience through the process. Patience is not one of Daniel's virtues. He is unable to see the need to wait for anything. The 'why', 'what' and 'when' is an even greater issue for him, as he is unable to ask the questions, let alone understand the answers. If we feel frustrated at our lack of control over a situation, he is likely to feel equally, if not more so and his behaviour will reflect that frustration. Daniel, and others with similar difficulties, present a more authentic version of the so-called norm, being unconstrained as they are by social niceties.

Chapter 6

CONCLUSIONS

The last twenty-seven years have been a steep learning curve for me. I have learned about disability in general, autism more specifically and, since Daniel's diagnosis three years ago, I am beginning to broaden my knowledge base to include Smith-Magenis Syndrome. My experience of Daniel plus the knowledge acquired through formal, structured study over the last twenty-seven years has helped me to make some sense of his behaviour in the context of his disability. However, this experience and knowledge cannot be applied retrospectively and so I dealt with situations I faced according to the level of understanding I had at the time, which looking back seems often painfully inadequate.

In relating some of the real life experiences through anecdotes, I am aware that my present knowledge would have explained so many things and with the benefit of hindsight I may have tackled some things differently. So many of my early concerns about Daniel's development were based on what I suppose is maternal instinct or intuition. I had no real knowledge against which to judge or challenge the views of the professionals involved in his life. I frequently felt that my judgement was being questioned, perhaps not deliberately, but it was enough to make me feel that I was being patronised or suggest that I was a neurotic mother. The G.P. dismissed my concerns on the basis that I was comparing Daniel with Matthew, the psychologist showed me how to play with him and I had to consistently press for a diagnosis, which no-one provided for years and years, yet so many of his characteristics or symptoms are recognised as features of either Autistic Spectrum Disorder or Smith-Magenis Syndrome.

In her book 'Children with Autism and Asperger's Syndrome'[4] Patricia Howlin states 'that the early babble of babies with autism is limited in range and complexity, that the pre-linguistic conversations between normal infants and their caretakers do not take place between babies with autism and their caretakers, that babies with autism do not lift up their arms to their parents in anticipation of being picked up, that they do not gurgle with delight if people smile or make noises to them and they do not attempt to initiate verbal interactions'. It is only recently that I have become aware of this through my study of autism, yet it was precisely the absence of all of the above in Daniel that concerned me and which I brought to the attention of the professionals when he was a baby.

His further problems with immune globulin deficiency, middle ear problems and gastric reflux have been connected with autism, although no conclusive research is yet available. His extreme dislike of having his hair brushed, washed or cut, his discomfort with hugs or touch generally, his disorientation caused by lasers at concerts, all indicate sensory sensitivity. His preference for tactile experiences and his obsessional behaviours are features which would not describe a person with learning difficulties alone, but one who was also on the autistic spectrum. Added to the above is the recent diagnosis of Smith-Magenis Syndrome. This condition was first described in 1983 in America when Daniel was aged seven. Of approximately thirty possible physical and behavioural characteristics to be found in someone with this condition, Daniel has at least twenty yet it was not until he was twenty-four that he was diagnosed, following the chance reading, by his houseparent in Scotland, of an article describing the condition.

I realise that it isn't possible for professionals to be completely up to date with the latest research but it is important that parents' observations are not ignored and that generalisations are not made about learning difficulties. In Daniel's case this masked the features of other disabilities and thus prevented appropriate diagnosis and consequential treatment.

As parents, we have been very grateful for the help and support of the professionals involved in Daniel's health and well being and would not dream of underestimating their expertise. However, while I'm sure they value the experience of parents I'm not so sure that they fully appreciate how much that parental experience could fill the many gaps in their knowledge of the child or adult they are dealing with. This has been particularly highlighted in our experiences with Daniel in hospitals and clinics. In these environments I have frequently found that my advice on Daniel's management has been dismissed, to his detriment.

The lack of appreciation by nurses, when I insisted that his arms must be held to prevent him from removing drips, caused him physical discomfort, as he had to have the process repeated more than once. It also delayed his recovery and subsequent discharge as it was often two hours or more before a doctor was available to carry out the procedure. There has sometimes also been a lack of recognition of the implications, both to the disabled person and the parents, of what to the staff may seem a straightforward course of action. A long wait to see the doctor or being told you have to go home and come back in two days time, may be unavoidable but it is not straightforward in terms of its implications when a learning disabled person is involved. It would help parents considerably if professionals acknowledged the difficulties a decision is likely to cause, even if that decision cannot be changed.

I felt acute frustration when, at a meeting of professionals, one of the therapists said he had discovered that Daniel responded well to music. Actually, I think frustrated is probably too mild a description of my feelings. When I asked why he hadn't sought some background information from us his response was that as Daniel is an adult, his therapy sessions are private. They are also a waste of time if people ignore the source of relevant information, in this case us, his parents, which might help in understanding their 'client' (I hate that word) and possibly in the planning and structure of the session. We could have told him that Daniel had been brought up with a wide variety of music and had responded very well in the past to music therapy.

I can almost hear the protests now from professionals claiming that they have always given parents the opportunity to participate in discussions concerning their child and I am sure they believe they have. However, being given permission to be involved is not always enough. There may be many reasons why some parents seemingly exclude themselves from participation, particularly those of an adult child. Historically, they may not have been used to being consulted or feel perhaps, like I did sometimes, that their opinions haven't been valued and therefore they believe that they have nothing useful to contribute.

I think it is sometimes inferred that because parents are so closely connected with their child that they can't 'see the wood for the trees'. There may be some truth in this. I'm sure that when I have felt completely overwhelmed with the stress of looking after Daniel I didn't necessarily have an objective view on the situation. In fact my wood often felt like a dense forest as I tried to maintain the juggling act of spinning plates in order to keep the balance within the family. However, this does not only apply to parents. I am also aware that those professionals who offer help and advice operate within their own forest of various theories and approaches, social policies and priorities, and budget of the time, and they may not necessarily see the wood for the trees either. It is probably the case that we are all trapped in our own subjectivity whilst rationalising about our objective approach to the situation, whatever it may be.

In the realm of learning difficulties, there is often considerable disparity between the developmental and chronological age of a person. I have to continually remind myself that Daniel is an adult who has twenty-seven years of his own life experience. Parents are often accused of being unable to 'let go' of their children and it is sad that there is such little understanding of the adjustments that have to be made by parents in order to cope with their child's transition to adulthood. I have spent years teaching and helping Daniel to do ordinary things such as feeding, washing and going to the toilet, all of which he still requires help with. I have taught him signs in order to communicate, taken him to numerous appointments, recreational activities and Church. In effect I have created what is for him his life and which to him is inseparable from me, not because I don't want to let him go, but because he is unable to see that life should be any different. Agreeing to let him go to a residential school in Scotland was the beginning of that process of separation, which has now progressed to his placement as an adult in a small group home. Everything that we have put in place so far has been for the purpose of preparing him for a life, which will eventually be without us. This effort will continue for as long as we are able to have any influence.

The bond with us, and the extended family, will always be strong but Daniel's connection with me seems to remain as it was when he was a child. When I collect him for his home visits he reverts immediately to his established pattern of behaviour that he associates with me, demanding absolute attention, and from which he seems unable to move on. Far from me not wanting to let him go, it is very much the opposite when he is in my company. Fortunately, my absence seems to trigger the 'off' switch, which enables him to get on with his life, with the constant support of his carers of course. This is some measure of reassurance as Linbert and I get older and we face the inevitability of our own mortality and the fact that we will probably not outlive our son. It is an ongoing source of concern that we will not always be here to look after his interests and we have to guard against the temptation of hoping that we will live longer than him so that we can take care of him to the end of his life. I know many parents who feel this way and who live with intense feelings of guilt caused by placing their child under a death wish.

If we felt confident about the notion of 'the community' that is promoted these days I imagine that we might be less concerned for Daniel's future. While we have to trust that he will be taken care of, we live with the underlying sense that society is not generally geared to protecting or enhancing the lives of the vulnerable and that the community into which Daniel is being encouraged can often be a very hostile place, especially for those who are 'different'. A pregnant woman today will be offered all manner of tests to detect whether her unborn baby is likely to have an abnormality. She is then left to make a decision to continue the pregnancy, perhaps in fear of the outcome, or to have a termination.

I do not intend to discuss the moral or ethical issues of such a debate but the fact that a choice is given to give or take a life says something about how society views the disabled person. Given that there is so much antagonism and selfishness in this world, it seems inconsistent that society is fearful of a child being produced who is unlikely to cause any deliberate hurt or who would do anything which would de-value another human being. This is not to say that I would wish disability on anyone, either personally or within a family. I would not.

My story of life with Daniel is some evidence of the sheer hard work, exhaustion and often desperation that is part of life with someone who needs a great deal of support. It is easy to become full of self-pity and feel that your life has been hijacked and is no longer your own. But of course, fundamentally, life is not our own. Life is for giving and sharing and if living with Daniel has given me more than an adequate opportunity for doing that, then he and I may have come somewhere close to our purpose. Sometimes people make glib comments such as 'you must be special to have been given a child like Daniel' and I have to exercise all the grace I can muster to be able to tell them that when I'm cleaning 'poo' off the bedroom walls at four in the morning, I don't feel terribly privileged.

I have to constantly remind myself of my own ignorance before I had Daniel and the fact that I might also have been tempted to make such comments. I try to be generous to people who have not been exposed to disability. However, dealing with ignorance, however innocent, is a constant challenge for me. People say things that are at best untrue and at worst very hurtful and while I feel committed to drawing their attention to something, I confess to not always having the presence of mind to say the right thing or the energy to pursue a discussion.

People generally have difficulty in coping with difference, either cultural, social, physical or intellectual. They feel comfortable with 'sameness' and sometimes judge others outside of their own blueprint as 'less than' rather than simply 'different'. In fact we are all one race and belong on the spectrum of humanity. Our variations are what makes life interesting and exciting – but clearly not to those who have a limited range of vision or who only accept those who fit their mould. Our idea of 'normal' usually includes physical appearance and ability, intelligence, personality and emotional stability thus making up a complete jigsaw. Anyone who is judged to be limited in any of these areas is likely to be viewed as an incomplete jigsaw.

So, for Daniel's future, do I trust that he will be valued and cared for by the community? One dictionary definition of community is 'a body of people in the same locality, leading a common life, having common rights and interests, sharing or owning in common with each other'. If these criteria were met, then one could suppose that the community was a supportive environment in which to live. In some older established communities this may be the case, but in these days it is quite possible that the only thing people have in common apart from their humanity, is where they live. The current social policy of Care in the Community is fine as long as there is a community in which to be cared for and it is one that meets the diverse needs of the people it is supposed to support.

The concept of community can mean different things to different people. It may suggest support to some, but for others the reality may be quite different.

With a divergence of opinion and understanding of community it is inevitable that there will also be a divergence of opinion and understanding of 'care'.

The approach towards normalisation and integration into society has given many disabled people greater independence as they have settled well into small group homes and are able to access local facilities. However, there are people, like Daniel, for whom access to such facilities would be better seen as an added extra rather than the primary objective of their care. The key word 'choice' features consistently in discussions concerning the lives of people who have learning difficulties.

We are constantly reminded that they have every right to choose what they do with their lives, and rightly so. But we are equally frustrated with this philosophy that ignores the fact that in order to make an informed choice one has to be able to process information. Daniel, and others like him, will never be able to make choices that require perceptual understanding. Choosing whether you live in a small house in the town or a large, spacious house in the country is not quite like choosing between beans or spaghetti. Our choice for Daniel, based on our experience of his life in Camphill and which we feel would best meet his needs, is a small community in a rural environment with enough land to have a few animals and a working garden.

However, now he is an adult our choice is not considered to be relevant and sadly this type of placement doesn't seem to rank very highly on the normalisation scale. I am not criticising the small, urban group home, which I believe is absolutely right for many people, but rather making the point that it should not be the sole provision, especially if the watchword is choice.

Diversity of needs requires a diversity of response and provision, which means giving proper consideration to what will contribute most to a person's quality of life. We live in a disorientated and often hostile society. It is possible that the kind of normal society that is being advocated, as the best place for people with learning difficulties to live, is being viewed through rose tinted spectacles. 'Normal' people choose to live in a variety of different ways, following their own interests and according to their own standards. This right should equally apply to people who have learning disabilities, who should not be expected to conform to other peoples' standards, but be able to set their own standard of normality, which will enrich their lives.

The late Dr Thomas Weihs[5] of the Camphill Movement said that the challenge was *'to find new forms of community living which will accept the individual, integral personality in such a way that the developmental 'otherness' becomes variety instead of abnormality - that diversity, rather than uniformity, becomes the foundation of healthy, social life.'*

These words by Dr Weihs were written many years ago but still apply today. We are a long way off that healthy social life but today people are continuing to rise to that challenge. Linbert and I have been married for thirty three years and for all of that time he has worked privately and professionally towards that ideal. In fact those two areas of life have been inseparable. We have personally been on the receiving end of prejudice in various forms, both subtle and overt and have a vested interest in helping to create a society that not only accepts, but values difference in people. Life has not always been easy but we have been privileged to have two lovely boys, who are very different from each other but equally loved and valued.

While Daniel demanded much attention, we tried hard to make sure our love for Matthew was apparent to him and that he was left in no doubt about his own 'specialness'. Like any family we had to be aware of each other's needs and made every effort to achieve balance in our relationships with each other but I guess during some of Daniel's 'extreme' moments we weren't always successful. We will always be grateful to Matthew for being so gracious (even if he didn't always feel like it) when he so often had to make way for Daniel. We will never forget the day when, at three years old, he clearly felt he had been unjustifiably nagged and announced *'you two don't deserve me.'* He was probably quite right on that occasion and could justifiably have said it many times since, but never did! We are just thankful that, far from resenting his lot in life, he has taken up the challenge to continue the work[6] that will lead to the kind of society in which everyone is valued and cared for.

Throughout our lives we have experienced some pain, many joys, many frustrations but always hope. At the conclusion of the story so far I have no need to be sad for I am in no doubt that Daniel was created for a purpose. Perhaps part of that purpose has been to help us, his close family, to find our own purpose. This is not to say that I believe we were given Daniel specifically to help us learn. That would be a very costly lesson, especially to him.

However, we have learned through him that humanity is a huge spectrum and people are individuals on it. We cannot be lumped together by race, nationality, colour, class, religion, gender or ability. We may have some common shared interests or characteristics, but we are very different and have different needs. We are all more than we appear to each other. Daniel is not just the sum total of his disabilities, he is a very real person, and as a Christian I believe he was created, as we all are, in the image of God who accords him absolute dignity and worth. We are grateful that he is part of our lives and will continue to do everything we can to ensure his security and provision for the future, trusting that God will always place in his path people who will value him for who he is, a very special person.

Finally – some very wise words from Thoreau.[7] *'If a man does not keep pace with his companions, perhaps it is because he hears a different drummer. Let him step to the music which he hears, however measured or far away.'*

REFERENCES

[1] For further information, contact:
The National Autistic Society
393 City Road
London
EC1V 1NG

[2] For further information, contact:
The Smith-Magenis Syndrome Foundation
www.smith-magenis.co.uk

[3] For further information, contact:
Botton Village – Camphill Village Trust
Danby
Whitby
North Yorks
YO21 2NJ

[4] Howlin P (1998) Children with Autism and Asperger
Syndrome.
Chichester: Wiley

[5] Weihs T Camphill Villages 1988

[6] Matthew and Emma commenced work as Salvation
Army Officers in May 2003

[7] Thoreau H D (1817-62) Walden (1854) 'Conclusion'